Christmas 1986 from Per &

W9-CIO-623

A Member of the Family
Letters and Reflections

by Dave Moore

A Member of the Family

Letters and Reflections

by Dave Moore

THE
LAZEAR
PRESS

Minneapolis/St. Paul
and Sante Fe

Author and Editor's note:

In the interest of maintaining the precise literary atmosphere of each letter, no grammatical, spelling or typographical errors have been eliminated from any of the original correspondence, including all of Mr. Moore's letters.

Copyright © 1986 by Dave Moore

All rights reserved

The Lazear Press is an imprint of The Lazear Agency Incorporated, Minneapolis and Santa Fe
3100 Ridgewood Circle
Orono, Minnesota 55356

Printed in the United States of America

First printing September 1986

10 9 8 7 6 5 4 3 2 1

Editors: Jonathon and Wendy Lazear
Art Direction: MacLean & Tuminelly
Cover and Text Design: Nancy MacLean
Production: Mike Tuminelly
Cover Photography: Tom Berthiaume
Back cover photos: Courtesy of WCCO-Television/Minneapolis-St. Paul and the *Minneapolis Star & Tribune*

Library of Congress Cataloging-in-Publication Number: LC 86-27099

ISBN: 0-9617423-0-5 (USA) hardcover

Table of Contents

Dedication

*To my employers and fellow employees of WCCO-TV,
past and present, for the patience and devotion that
have kept me afloat long enough to have collected the
bounty herein.*

Publisher's Note

Where possible, permission has been received from each of the correspondents to publish their letters. In those cases where the letter is of an inflammatory nature, or in other ways might cause embarrassment to the writer, we have used only the writer's initials. The addresses of the writers have been deleted. To all of the writers the author and publishers express our genuine appreciation and gratitude, for without them there would be no book.

Preface

First, a disclaimer: What we have here is neither autobiography, instructional tome, anecdotage, formal history, blasphemy, confessional, nor a loving or critical analysis.

Some of all those elements are present. For want of a better phrase, it is an Epistolary Collective: letters from the public, gathered over a period of time, to a television newscaster, together with his responses.

I began stashing away such correspondence in the mid-sixties at the suggestion of a sociology Ph.D. candidate fascinated by the public's attachment to the television newscast, which, at the time, was the mirror of that era of tremendous domestic and social unrest that has permeated the years and touched all of us.

Jonathon and Wendy Lazear, successful literary agents (turned publishers for this occasion and I wish them well) are convinced that such a collection, gathered by one who has toiled in the vineyards for nearly thirty years, would serve not only the public's curiosity, but also, if only to a trivial degree, scholars of mass communication.

In the early fifties, the local television newscast was a deterrent to the profitability of a broadcasting operation. Even though it was beginning its fight for respect and recognition in the community, it was yet a specie only to be tolerated by management. But in the Twin Cities community it was more than just tolerated by one, Stanley Hubbard. In 1948 his KSTP operation, long an innovator in radio broadcast news, became Minneapolis/St. Paul's first licensed television station, and at once, under Hubbard's mercurial leadership, his news operation became a community force, setting the standard for the quick-striking, fast-paced, spirited television newscast that preceded the era of the more contrived, fancifully produced news program of today.

Paradoxically, the newscaster Hubbard selected to ride herd on the meteor-like program was a man of gentle mien. The calming presence of Bill Ingram served as assurance to the thousands of families gathered before their television sets each evening at ten o'clock — a time slot the legendary Cedric Adams had established on WCCO radio in the thirties — that the world was not on the brink. Resonant of tone, and with a comforting manner similar to that of the fabled Adams, Ingram was welcomed into the homes as a member of those same families who had developed so lasting a kinship and affection for Adams. Even more ingratiating was Ingram's custom of signing off each fifteen minute newscast with a confiding wink and a salutory smile.

Through the years I have forecast, inaccurately, as it seems to be turning out, the gradual decline of the studio newscaster. The astonishing progress of the capabilities of electronic journalism, whereby news events are reported "live," on the spot as they occur, would, in due time, it had seemed to me, render obsolete a mere person, seated behind a mere desk, away from the scene of action.

To my personal gratification quite the opposite has happened. In the fifties, while Ingram's wink was seducing families in the Twin Cities, John Cameron Swayze's "hop-Scotching around the world" was becoming household nationally. In the turbulent sixties, millions of families across the country willingly suspended belief to accept Walter Cronkite's "that's the way it is" signoff as paternal assurance, an audiovisual transmission of trust, integrity and — the quality that has come to be the optimum measurement of a newscaster's worth — credibility.

Twenty eight years of reading the day's news into a machine each evening at ten o'clock seems to have assured my inclusion in this social phenomenon. "Institution," "a member of the family," "influential," "credible," and as I approach dotage, "avuncular" and "patriarchal" are words that have been ascribed to my television persona.

I do not find such words pejorative. They are the rewards of longevity. They are gratifying, and, I fear, humbling. Each of us welcomes acceptance. But while many strive for it, plan their lives to bring it about, agonize over it and even connive for it, I seem to have acquired it by merely showing up, time and again. A fortunate circumstance, rare for one of a singular — ah! but marketable — talent such as mine. With this book, I intend to neither abuse acceptance nor glorify it, but merely to point it out as the genesis of this collection of correspondence.

A word here of my employers who have been most responsible for my durability. As the facade of a television newscast, as the manufacture and packaging of its elements — including the grating, folksy, family team approach — in short, as style appears to have gained priority over substance, so, too has the anxiety level of the broadcast executive in his constant search for "presentable" on-the-air people. "Presentable" is determined by the audience "ratings," that intimidating, life-threatening hoax, whereby a survey of one thousand viewers claims to accurately determine which television programs five-hundred-thousand people watch.

Statisticians and pollsters swear the system is irrefutable. Right or wrong, it is a ruthless force that imposes on those in its grasp a riveting peril. Few other professions are possessed by such a villainous, albeit superficial, threat.

Who knows the number of families broken, careers destroyed by this merciless concept, pandered to by thousands of management people of otherwise undeniable intelligence?

My employers over these thirty years — actually two sets of management — have been the rare exception. Certainly they have respected the audience survey ratings, as Fay Wray and later Jessica Lange respected King Kong, and like those two movie heroines, have refused to be cowered by them. Otherwise many years ago either Eau Claire or Sioux Falls would have become my workplace.

Indeed, there was a long, dreary period of time during the seventies when WCCO-TV fought desperately just to hang on to second place, a disgrace not to be tolerated even by the most patient of executives. At no time during that trying period did management imply that my position was in jeopardy. Nor was it ever suggested, that to improve my persona (image?) I make alterations in style or grooming. I was left alone — to grow in the job, and then to grow old in the job.

So what have we here? It is unlikely that fifty years from now some social historian will use this volume as a research tool to examine late twentieth century mores and thought. It may, however, serve as a microcosm not only of a public expression and reaction to affairs of the day — running deeper than the stern objectivity of computerized opinion polls and surveys — but to demonstrate to

5

what degree citizens in the privacy of their homes have reacted to the hazards and joys of the day as reported to them by another citizen, the newscaster. So convivial is this otherwise simple social alliance, that I am almost hesitant to point out that it has produced an embarrassing complication: much of the viewing public perceives the newscaster's position as a lofty one, rife with omniscience and expertise in such complex subjects as urban affairs, school funding, farm and labor relations. I'm sure the implication will be apparent in some of the letters in this book.

In the editing and selection process the Lazears and I discovered I do not come off well in many of these exchanges. For one who is thought to be of generally good cheer and fair mind, I am chagrined to find that even while only mildly vexed, my responsive manner has been, more than occasionally, bitter, abrasive, unduly defensive and downright rude. To apologize here, belatedly, would be to retract personal convictions which, at the time, required sting. Oh, how I envy those with the verbal wherewithal to distinguish acerbity from gracelessness! I am not in the least comforted by editors of famous letter writers, such as Woolf, Thurber, James, and Fred Allen, who claim that as one ages so do his levels of intolerance and grouchiness rise. I find neither comfort nor merit in aging. But for all my cantankerousness, a number of my replies contain a degree of humility, admitted guilt and acknowledged error. Over all these years, the unthinking, offhanded, cutesy ad-lib has been returned to me by perceptive, intelligent, sensitive citizens unwilling to accept callousness and flippancy with their daily news reports. To such letters I have responded with head bowed and reassured — as all of us in this work must be from time to time — that it is not an altogether unthinking public out there.

It is also a public that is anxious to share. The casual dropping — during a newscast — of the name of a long-gone local athlete or politician, has moved older citizens to write of personal remembrances of days still in crisp focus.

How little it must be known to all of them — not only the outraged and the elderly, but the adolescent, the teenager, the college student, the educator, the professional, the institutionalized, the welfare recipient, the public servant, the scorned and the blessed of all age and gender — that their letters have provided the newscaster with a view through a window to our time, privileged by very few, if indeed, any.

What we have here then is the kind of thing Studs Terkel has done so well, without the tape recorder: an informal, unschooled expression of our time and place from those who give to time and place a special ambience.

Had he read this book I wonder if it would have changed Thoreau's mind about letter writing. In *Walden II* he wrote, "I have received no more than two letters in my life that were worth the postage."

I grieve that perfection of the long distance telephone has put letter writing on the wane. There are recent publications to remind us of how satisfying a pastime it has been: Shaw's letters to Mrs. Patrick Campbell; the letters of E.B. White, Virginia Woolf and Harry Truman. These volumes illuminate the centuries-old truism, "More than kisses, letters mingle souls."

I hope you'll find that true here.

1

What is News — What is Not News

Years ago when I posed that question to a fourth grader, he replied, "News is what just happened."

Horace Greeley, Walt Whitman, H.L. Mencken, Joseph Pulitzer, Eric Sevareid and George Will are among the several hundred thousand professionals who have taken a stab at the question. I favor Sevareid's definition which I have paraphrased:

*"Bad news is what is news when one assumes normalcy.
If one were to assume nothing but upheaval — in short,
if upheaval were normal — then only GOOD news
would be THE news."*

To further complicate the puzzlement I advance the theory of Perceptual Selection, by which we dismiss or embrace certain attitudes and prejudices that are inherent in all of us; attitudes and prejudices that influence that which we retain, that which we forget.

Following a particular newscast on a February night of 1972, a call from a St. Paul viewer could not have come at a more propitious time since I was preparing a talk on this very question for a journalism seminar. The notes I have salvaged from that telephone conversation (and of course, subsequently, put to good use in the talk) take us as close as we can get to defining Perceptual Selection.

The viewer had called to express her abhorrence of our "negative" treatment of young people, a condition to which we had been prone for a long time, she claimed, but tonight we had reached the apex.

Indeed, within the body of the newscast were such items as young radicals vandalizing a University building; four teenagers arrested in a narcotics raid; young people embarked for Cuba to help harvest Fidel Castro's grain crop. As stable as was her retention, in detail, of those "negative" items, vague was her retention — in the same newscast, remember — of our coverage of a ceremony in Edina in which three brothers received Eagle Scout badges; volunteer high schoolers working with handicapped children at Project Head Start; St. Catherine students acting as "seeing eyes" for residents at a home for the blind in St. Paul.

Thus we have both the Sevareid and the Perceptual Selection theories at work here: News that is retained or memorable, is news of upheaval, "bad" news. News that is a reflection of normalcy, or "good" news, is neither memorable, nor so easily retained, since there is nothing exceptional about it.

To further complicate the issue, a television newscast, unlike a newspaper, is bound by time constrictions that demand an edited, moving picture, as well as condensed, salient facts.

The following letters provide further insight into these and related issues.

May 3, 1983

Re: Improving the 10 O'clock News

Dear Dave:
Channel 4's news at 10:00 P.M. is laboring ineffectively just as are the other stations. The amount of real news presented is so slight that the viewer who would like to get a news summary at that time is sorely disappointed. It is a rare evening when WCCO has significant news other than accidents and fire which cover more than eight of the thirty minutes. Then comes a contrived "human interest" story of made-up news followed by five to ten minutes of clowning about the weather which could be presented in thirty seconds. The session ends with a prolonged reading of the daily athletic scores. For a person who does not have time to listen to the news at other times during the day this is very meager fare.

One area of news which I find is covered little, if at all, is reporting from our own Congressmen and Senators in Washington regarding their activities and the bills which they are working for. Even though Skip Loescher is in Washington, I cannot remember a time since the last election when one of our own Representatives or Senators from Minnesota appeared to present his point of view.

I suggest that one evening a week for ten minutes on the 10 o'clock news you invite in rotation our eight Representatives and two Senators to spend ten minutes presenting his activities and his analysis of the significant activities on which he is working. I would urge that this not be a contrived session in which the Congressman or Senator was obliged to respond to questions, but, rather, a period in which the Congressman could organize and present his information in an orderly fashion with the emphasis on those things that he thinks are most important. This would be a marked departure from current newscasting. It would allow us to see how each of the Congressmen and Senators approaches the significant problems of the day. It would focus our attention on those problems as our Senators and Congressman saw their importance. It would help us to understand and judge the effectiveness of our representatives in Congress. Most of all, I think that it would become one of the outstanding weekly aspects of the 10 o'clock news and attract a considerable amount of attention.

By inviting each Congressman and each Senator in rotation, this would spread the activity over ten weeks. If you asked the Governor and the Mayors of Minneapolis and St. Paul to participate in the series you would have a thirteen week schedule and have each speaker participating only four times per year. That is really a very infrequent time for each of these men when one considers the magnitude of their public responsiblities. However, it would be a great advance over anything that we have at the present time. By allowing each speaker to organize his own presentation according to what he thought was most important to present to the people, this would make a bona fide Minnesota forum of political information. I think that the Congressmen, who do not get as much chance as they would like to communicate with the people, would appreciate the opportunity and that the listening audience would be highly responsive to such a program.

I am writing to you regarding this proposal because over the years you have been one of our outstanding newscasters with a deep concern toward making the dissemination of news a meaningful educational process. I hope that through this suggestion it will be possible to add a weekly component of education on political issues which will be both beneficial and attractive to the viewing public.

Sincerely,

F. J. Kottke

Frederic J. Kottke, M.D.

May 6, 1983

Dear Dr. Kottke,

Your suggestion shows perception and a good deal of thought, and I thank you for taking the time to detail it as thoroughly as you have.

Ideally, a ten minute discussion with one of our elected representatives one night each week at 10 PM would be suitable for a one hour newscast. For our limited time span of thirty minutes, however, it is impractical.

You are aware, I'm sure, that whenever an issue warrants, Skip Loescher or Jim Gately of our Washington bureau, do, indeed, talk with one of our Senators or Congressmen. Off hand I would say this happens two or three times each week at ten, but briefly, to be sure, and more frequently on our 5 PM Reports.

I am assuming that your suggestion that ten minutes once each week would preclude those shorter, more frequent interviews. If so, we would not have the benefit of the Congressman's ideas at that particular moment, concerning that particular issue.

Frankly, I should like to see one of our 10 PM Reports extended to one hour, one night each week to accommodate your suggestion. At any rate I will pass your letter along to our News Director, Reid Johnson, for his consideration.

While your suggestion is a viable one, I hasten to correct you on the premise that inspired the suggestion.

Generally our weather reports do not run five minutes in length — unless, of course, extreme conditions warrant it. The prescribed time for our weather segments is <u>three</u> minutes. No more. And that does not allow for "clowning."

For those who are not interested in such things — and I admit there are times when I must include myself there — the three minutes may <u>seem</u> considerably longer.

Again, I thank you for taking the time to write. I would like to think there will be a day when your suggestion, or something akin to it, will be implemented into our 10 PM newscasts.

Sincerely,

Dave Moore

Dear Mr. Moore,

I have been thinking about writing to you for months. Ever since you had the report on tv about institutions (state) for the retarded.

I found your report and film coverage to be very colorless and with no kind of positive support for the valuable services and activities state institutions offer retarded residents.

Institutional living is not all good, nor is it all bad. And I for one would like to see your ch. 4 news team give some coverage to the positive side of institutional living for the retarded.

Abuse of other human beings has sadly been going on since time began — it happens in homes, in schools, on street corners, in parks, in prisons, in institutions, in nursing homes, in group homes, everywhere there are people. I realize that this abuse makes for "news" and I guess that in itself makes a real statement about what society wants to hear on t.v. news programs. Good news hasn't had a history of selling news programs, has it? And isn't that tragic!

I am asking you to charge right out and make a change in the total picture of the news you cover — I am asking you to take a risk and report something positive — in particular, about institutional living for the retarded.

Send your news team out to the state institutions — look for happy people, wonderful volunteer programs, fun parties, dances, picnics, educational and work programs, on staff medical services, companionship, a place retarded people can call home.

For many reasons, state institutions are the only option some retarded people have to call home. In all fairness to those people, their families and the people who care about them, I think ch. 4 news should give some time to whats right about state institutions.

You and your news team strike me as being the kind of people who are willing to take chances — Are you willing to report good news for a change?

I might add that I have no retarded child. I have several retarded friends who do not live in a state institution. My interest in this matter of what's right about state institutions comes from a long association with the idea that there is good everywhere if people will take the time to look for it.

I trust that you and your news team will give my letter some serious thought.

Sincerely,

Sue Odette

Sue Odette

October 26, 1983

Dear Ms. Odette,

It is never easy to define "news." What is News? What is not News?

Journalists and sociologists and historians have generally agreed that "news" is what is not of the norm; that which is counter to our every day living. Murder in a community is news because it is not a normal condition. The deaths of 5 people in an automobile accident is not a normal condition; therefore it is "news."

Thus in response to your sensitive and, I must say, very eloquent perceptions, "volunteer programs, fun parties, dances, picnics, educational and work programs" are not news. We must assume that those circumstances are a part of the day-to-day conditions of life in a state institution.

BUT when abuses take place in those institutions (taxpayer supported institutions) we have news because they are NOT a part of the day-to-day conditions.

I hope that in some way this satisfies your inquiry, although I fear not.

Sincerely,

Dave Moore

_____

Feb. 10, 1972

Dear Mr. Moore:

I have about had it with that evening dose of "hogwash" by Al Austen. His comments about the Kunstler thing were out of order, uncalled for, and not very well thought out.

You have a fine program, and I am most happy to extend the privilege of coming into my living room. Please do not abuse that privilege by forcing me to swallow someone elses political opinions.

If the station wants this sort of thing, why not bring him on at the very last, and it will be easy to switch chanels and not miss any of the rest of your program.

I can't help but believe I'm just one of many who don't care for this feature of your program.

Sincerely,

Louis J. LaMere

February 11, 1972

Dear Mr. LaMere,

Your complaint regarding Al Austin's recent editorial remarks on William Kunstler's prohibited appearance at the Rochester Junior College, indicates a lack of familiarity with the concept of editorialism.

It is not Mr. Austin's function to accomodate his editorial comment to whatever popular feeling may prevail at the time, but rather to: (1) call attention to an issue or cause that may have escaped the public's notice (2) support a cause or issue which is felt merits support (3) take a stand against an issue or cause which is felt to be inequitable or unjust.

Both Mr. Austin and his employers (WCCO-TV) feel that prohibiting Mr. Kunstler from speaking is not only an unjust action against those who may wish to hear him, but an unequivocal violation of the "free speech" concept of our Constitution.

It is our feeling that when one person, no matter what his or her political or social ideology, is prevented from speaking to a public gathering, the enforcers of such action have committed a crime far more heinous than those who are not allowed to speak.

Mr. Austin did not request approval of Mr. Kunstler's philosophy, only that he be allowed to state his philosophy, so that others of us who have not heard him may make our own decisions.

Sincerely,

Dave Moore

June 15, 1972

Dear Mr. Moore:

Recently you commented on the poll your WCCO had had taken of a number of Minnesotans. The poll referred to attitudes toward the release of prisoners of North Vietnam.

The data indicated that a large proportion of Minnesotans *do not think the North Vietnamese will release American prisoners when the war is over.*

It is a sad fact that the American people are the most poorly informed of all the so-called advanced peoples of the world. That they are so may be due to our poor educational system, which does not educate, but even more perhaps to our communication systems which are agents of propoganda rather than purveyors of news or information that is factual and educative.

You, therefore, should not be surprised at the poor state of information among Minnesotans, which I have learned is not greater than that among natives and citizens of other states - as I have lived in several states during my life.

As a matter of fact, anyone who reads history would know that prisoners of war are not released until the war is ended. They have not been, and I imagine they will not be. I would suggest that if you at WCCO were to do your proper job you would have so informed the people who listen to you, and then the numbers on the poll would have been significantly different. Perhaps, even, a majority may have been aware of this fact about war prisoners.

You still, for example, use the word "Communists" when referring to the North Vietnamese. Which is propaganda pure and simple — and it is the bunk as you may well know, though if you don't, why are you the news communicator at WCCO? It may be that we have press editors and the more verbal news passers who are not any better informed than their readers or hearers — in which case, it is clear why we Americans are so poorly informed about almost anything.

I had thought the object of communication was to educate and to inform. It seems I am wrong; *the object of communication is to keep people ignorant.* I've listened to you much of recent years. You may be a bit better than your

17

competitors but trivially. I wish we had some way the people could be given genuine information . . .

You spout about the "aggression" of The North Vietnamese against the South Vietnamese!!! Remember the Geneva agreement and who prevented the unity of the country and a free election??? And then who is the aggressor? Who are the foreigners in Vietnam? And who are the people hated by both the surviving people of North and South Vietnam?

But neither the radio, nor the TV nor the press makes any effort to inform the American people of the facts. All you do is pass on the bunk.

And, my dear friend, you are beginning to get a snarl on your otherwise nice face when you speak the word "Communist." If not on your face, in your voice. The snarl is there. I suppose you will go on doing it, and I will go on feeling nauseated by your betrayal of truth and by the way our communication industry has prostituted itself to the government and the military brain washers.

Sincerely yours,

Emerson W. Harris

Emerson W. Harris
Minister

June 19, 1972

Dear Mr. Harris,
Although I may not have learned the nomenclature of international political science, succinctness is a working peculiarity of my vocation, and since your arrogance and presumptuousness seem to be exceeded only by your long-windedness, I shall try to be as brief as the limits of my patience will allow.

#1) I am sure you have misstated your challenge to poll in question. You say our poll showed a "large proportion of Minnesotans do not think the North Vietnamese will release American prisoners when the war is over.

Later you state: "prisoners of war are not released until the war is ended. They have not been and I imagine they will not be." So? Those surveyed apparently feel that even when the war is ended, the prisoners will not be released. I fail to see how that proves we have not done our "proper job." Somehow, in your zeal to take us to task, you have mis-written what you had to mind.

#2) In the past we have been guilty of using the word "communist" with reference to the North Vietnamese. Recognizing the error, we have tried to correct it. On those rare occasions when it slips through, I am at fault. It is a part of my job to check for it and delete it because it is an inaccurate description.

#3) We do not "spout about the aggression of the North Vietnamese against the South Vietnamese." Indeed, we are just as appalled as you, I'm sure, by the administration's use of the word "aggression" with reference to the North Vietnamese, and its use of the phrase "protective reaction" when the US is clearly the aggressor.

#4) There is no "snarl" on my face or in my voice when I read the word "communist," nor is the object of communications to "keep the people ignorant." While I take umbrage to such scurillous charges, I am willing to recognize that they are products of ignorance and over-zealousness, both forgiveable ingredients of human frailty. I am disappointed, however, that a man of God is incapable of being similarly disposed toward human error, of which I admit to having been professionally guilty more than once.

Sincerely,

Dave Moore

June 22, 1972

Dear Mr/ Moore:

During the past year and a half I have written to the news staff of WCCO at least three times, possibly more often; to you, to Mr. Loescher, to Mr. Austin. These letters were courteous, thoughtful, midly critical and far less

19

mildly complimentary. In response — silence. I decided to see what a nastily written letter might accomplish — a reply. Success! My letter was not ignored as were the others. And a reply to two pages!!!

As to #2, I wrote sometime ago about. The misuse of the word "communism" and noticed that for a time thereafter, you seldom used the word in deference to the North Vietnamese. Lately, however, you have begun using the word far more often. You see: I Listen to you.

As to #3. Has there not been a noticeable softening of attitude with respect to Mr. Nixon and the war? Have not Mr. Agnew's fulminations had some effect? And not just with you and your staff members, but even Mr. Cronkite has changed. Time and again you have referred to "agreession" by the North against the south. Is not this spouting what Mr. Nixon, Mr. Laird, and the Pentagon want the news media to spout? Or were my ears hearing incorrectly?

As to #1, As I recall your poll indicated the majority did not think the American war prisoners would not be released when the war is over — if it ever is. My comment is that this indicates that the news media has not done its job adquately. Mr. Nixon, and before him, Mr. Johnson, stated that upon release of the prisoners, we would stop fighting. My comment is that Mr. Johnson and Mr. Nixom are misleading the American people. Prisoners of war are not normally released until the war is over and the peace treaty signed, and in the normal peace treaty is provision for return of prisoners. The fact that so many Americans are not, or seem not aware of this, indicates that someone has done a poor job of informing the citizens. Let us grant that our schools do a good job /in a few respects, and a very poor job in others. But it is the newes media whose responsibility it is to inform the people. AND I say that had WCCO, KSTP, etc, and the *Tribune,* and *Post Dispatch* and their fellows in other communities and states done their job properly, the citizens would think differently. That is the point I make.

Of course I may be an "ignorant" cuss, lacking in the ordinary social amenities. I do not deny this. I have only read something over twenty thousand volumes during the course of my li/fe, covering history, economics, art, politics, social issues, biography, mystery, adventure, exploration, the various sciences, and even a few on the subject of religion. I now read only some thirty journals of opinion of various shades, every month. I make no claim to be other than ignorant. So I am not offended by your defensive comments. Had you and your friends responded to my other letters, I would not have written so nastily. Anyway, my letter got noticed and read. For which I thank you. Normally you fellows do a good job and I am not normally critical of you. I just think that the lack of information on the part of the people generally ought to be laid at someone's feet and where other than the news media?

After all, some years ago, a study revealed that the average American read not more than three books a year. Sad.

Anyway thanks for your noticing my letter.

Emerson W. Harris
Emerson W. Harris

If your interest in the "ethics" of journalism is only casual, or not at all, I suggest you move on to the next chapter. The complex nature of this subject requires a bit more space than we will devote to others.

There was a time when the Battle of Journalism Ethics was fought intramurally — within the profession. But within recent years it has become a public issue. Certainly ethics was the focal point of the famous Wesbrook Pegler - Quentin Reynolds libel case of the thirties, but Watergate, the Daniel Ellsberg/Pentagon Papers, Westmoreland vs. CBS, Sharon vs. Time Magazine all brought the question into the public arena.

Principals in the foregoing correspondence are a well-known Minneapolis attorney-politician, and Lou Gelfand, the Ombudsman (reader's representative) for the *Minneapolis Star/Tribune*.

To curb, somewhat, the length of the matter, I have employed some judicious editing.

Editor
St. Paul Dispatch & Pioneer Press
55 East Fourth Street St.
Paul, MN 55101

Dear Sir:
Last week, your newspaper published an article concerning the shoplifting conviction of Lieutenant Governor candidate Marlene Johnson. The manner in which that story was handled demonstrated a complete lack of integrity. I am compelled to protest your breach of trust in revealing the identity of a confidential source.

Dan Cohen, a former public official and contributing editor to the *Minneapolis Star* newspaper, who understands well the integrity of a free press, made available to your reporter documented court records of Ms. Johnson's arrest history and conviction. That information had not previously been brought to the attention of the public, although it was easily available. Mr. Cohen felt that especially in an election year, facts relevant to a candidate's past or present fitness should be divulged and discussed before people voted on the qualifications of that person for public office. It would make little or no sense to discuss it after the election.

Mr. Cohen brought these documents to your reporter and your newspaper with the absolute and clearly stated condition that he not be revealed as the source of this information and that he remain anonymous. He requested and was promised anonymity. Subsequent to that promise and assurance and after he delivered the information to your reporter, he was then informed by that same reporter that your paper had decided to reveal him as the source and that the story was going to be printed with that information.

Mr. Cohen refused to negotiate on the release of your pledge of anonymity and once again informed your reporter that he had not and would not give permission to have his name used to be revealed as the source of the information. At no time was Mr. Cohen given the opportunity to withdraw information he had given to the reporter so as to protect his anonymity. Your paper then saw fit to violate the absolute anonymity which had been promised and proceeded to publish the article, revealing Mr. Cohen as the source of the information.

Mr. Cohen was fired from his job because his name appeared in that particular story and he has been subjected to public embarrassment and ridicule. For what reason? Surely, your paper did not need to breach its agreement with Mr. Cohen in order to confirm the veracity of the factual data which he gave to you. A minimal amount of investigation by any of your reporters would have revealed that the information was correct without breaking a promise and the breach of trust. By taking this action, you have compromised journalistic integrity.

A newspaper builds it reputation based on credibility and trust. Your betrayal of trust in this case is reprehensible, not just because it was unnecessary, but for the chilling effect it will and ought to have on anyone who might think they could trust the integrity of your newspaper, rely on promises, and be protected as a confidential source. You have given the public fair warning that source confidentiality and promises of anonymity cannot compete with expediency.

Very truly yours,

Gary W. Flakne

Although Mr. Flakne's letter was addressed to the *St. Paul Dispatch-Pioneer Press,* the story broke in the *Minneapolis Star and Tribune.* That newspaper's Ombudsman, Lou Gelfand, after publishing the comments of several readers, offered comments in two Sunday issues of that paper, on November 7 and November 21, 1982.

Lou Gelfand, The Star and Tribune:
November 7, 1982

In my view, for this newspaper to have published the information without the source would have jeopardized its credibility to the reader. Publishing Cohen's name without his permission is justified by an unspoken standard of journalism that defines the substance of Cohen's tip as beneath the threshold of acceptable, unattributable information.

November 21, 1982

The confrontation is based on different perceptions of what constitutes a confidence. The perceptions come from equally honest and honorable bases.

I've concluded that Cohen, because of his twenty-year relationship with the news media, must have shared some of the editors' perception of what constitutes a confidence: that the editor's assumption of Cohen's news media know-how was a strong factor in their decision, and that the October 28th article should have included an explanation of the confidentiality Cohen was promised and why it was not honored.

November 9, 1982

Dear Dave:

Enclosed please find a copy of a letter I wrote last week to the *Minneapolis Star-Tribune,* and a copy of the response from the Sunday, November 7th issue of that newspaper with the by-line of Lou Gelfand.

As a lay person who has dealt for over twenty years with both the written and electronic media, it is my understanding that the confidentiality of a source was a basic tenet of the journalistic profession. In reading Mr. Gelfand's comments, he makes reference to "unspoken standards" of journalism. Apparently, the failure to meet these "standards" allows the revealing of a source.

I would appreciate your perusing the two enclosures in the context of this "unspoken standard." There is some confusion and misunderstanding with the ethics involved in revealing a source where there is only an unspoken standard for the lay person, reporter or editor to use as a guide.

Might I please have your comments or your suggestions where a person might turn to obtain some objective criteria and also your thoughts on this "standard." If it is inconvenient for you to correspond with me, I will make a contact with you in the hopes of obtaining more information on this issue.

Thank you for any consideration you can give me on my request.

Very truly yours,

Gary W. Flakne

November 12, 1982

Dear Gary:

I have my own "standards":

If a source, who wished to remain anonymous, revealed to me information I felt viable and to the public good, I would accept the information — after checking it out — use it, but not the source's name.

If I felt the information to be frivolous, insignificant, and (to be more specific) offered as a desperation measure in a political campaign — such as I felt about the Marlene Johnson information — I would not accept it.....IF the source insisted on anonymity.

I might use the information if the source approved use of his name. In this case I felt the source of the information to be more newsworthy than the information.

I am not aware of an "unspoken standard of journalism." It seems to me if it's "unspoken," it does not exist.

Regards,

Dave Moore

Dear Mr. Moore

The thoughts I am about to share with you are sincere and I invite you to reflect about them deeply and frequently.

I now turn Channel 4 off when it comes to News Time and for one reason: your constant emphasis on being the best and/or number one. We are living in a society where there is *too much emphasis* on being #1. I am a parent of three, ages seventeen, twenty and twenty-four. I hope I have related to them and others that there is room in life for all and being #1 or best or Nielson ratings (a menace to self-esteem) achievement is not the only factor in life. This is not the same as not working hard, acheiving, setting goals.

A few years ago when I was in Minneapolis (something I avoid) I was in an elevator with you and we were both going to a Press lunch. I was very turned off by your feeling that news is a responsibility no matter who it hurts etc. — *You and other media people* need to re-evaluate what news means. There is room for more GOOD NEWS —

Sincerely,

Mrs. Nancy J. Slater

Mrs. Nancy J. Slater

November 3, 1982

Dear Ms. Slater:

In response to your letter, I wish you to know that over the past dozen years or so, I have focused talks to school groups — elementary, high school, and college — on the damage our country's obsession with "Number One-ism" has imposed on the quality and credibility of television journalism.

The fierce competition to win the most viewers — to be #1 — is not only repugnant to me, but the fact that the inspiration for such fanaticism is born of an entirely false concept, the audience rating surveys, compounds my abhorence of the situation.

26

Many of my colleagues feel as I do. But we also realize that the drive to be "number one" is an inexplicable part of the competitive, free enterprise system. I am sure each of us — no matter what our profession — is displeased by certain conditions of our work. But we do not forsake the work because a personal ideal has been abused by it, especially when all other conditions of the work are favorable. One of the favorable conditions in my case is that my employers neither condemn my speaking out on this matter, nor oppose my writing the kind of letter I am writing to you.

As to your vague reference to my elevator conversation you overheard "a few years ago," I suggest that the elapsed time may have fogged your recall: never, never have I ever felt that "news is a responsibility, no matter whom it hurts etc."

I was both embarrassed and appalled by our handling of the Judge Crane Winton incident. But again, that is a personal view, and one, judging by our mail on the matter, not shared by all others.

I agree there is room for "good news," and while it may not abound on our newscasts, neither is it obscured. Breakthroughs in medical science, and positive changes in consumer, ecological, and public safety development, are reported regularly and accurately.

I am neither expectant that nor interested in this response returning you to channel 4. I merely wished to set the record straight.

Sincerely,

Dave Moore

January 10, 1984

Dear Mr. Moore,

I have been a fan of yours for many years and a regular viewer of your 10 p.m. news. I recognize there is a great deal of competition between the networks for popularity—the ratings. I am sorry to say that your "new" format leaves me cold. Your "one back offense" with your cohorts checking in on miniature screens lacks warmth—the personal, face-to-face interplay you had before. Not only is it gimmicky but your topics are so capsulized in tiny segments that even the commercials seem big by comparison. I think it is ironical that all your modern techology has not led to better news coverage but far worse. Your program Monday 1/9 had a thirty sec. opener and your modern station swung immediately to an Old Dutch potato chip. As an experienced actor, you know this is not good theatre. Hope you do something to convince your station that humaness is vital too.

Floyd Pearson

January 18, 1984

Dear Mr. Pearson,

I'm sorry; I appreciate your comments, but you are a little late.

As the new technology and the gimmickry became increasingly abhorrent to me, I screamed and kicked my feet and wrote memos and letters and gave speeches and now I am tired and have directed my attention to doing the best job I can under the circumstances.

In a sense, come to think of it, I am not interested in restoring that "face-to-face interplay" you seemed to have enjoyed. I want to get back to the old fashioned business of getting the news on the air — I am not interested in sitting around making small talk with my colleagues.

For the little good it will do, I passed your comments along to our News Director. And I thank you for taking the time to write.

Sincerely,

Dave Moore

In late 1982 our marketing people implanted the label, "News for Thinking People."

July 13, 1983

Dear Mr. Moore,

As a consistent viewer of the Channel 4, 10 PM news, I must comment on last night's (Tuesday 7/12) show. Do you believe that program, and many others in recent weeks, really are for "The Thinking Man?"

The *lead* story was another *seven* minutes on the Elk River tragedy!

What seems like forever was the "expose" that bikes are stolen when left unlocked!

Only a few seconds on Senator Durenberger and a serious health insurance problem and two short stories about jobs leaving Minnesota. Was there any domestic news?

No foreign news, no IDS acquisition, no increase in Prudential jobs — sadly very little substance. I like the short, to the point weather segment, Pat Miles is attractive and probably has something to say, your ending stories are cute and fun, the sports reports are OK — but to call your show "The Thinking Man's" news — hardly.

Sadly, but sincerely yours

Joel Levine

Joel Levine

July 19, 1983

Dear Mr. Levine,
I'm with you 100%!
Since the day it was invoked last October I have personally fought (to no avail, of course) the presumptous "thinking people" theme.
As everyone knows it establishes a standard that no television newcast — including those of the network —

can accommodate. Besides, it discriminates against those of us who <u>don't</u> think.

As to the long "exposes" (bicycle thievery, etc.) it is the bane of all newscasters and producers. It is frustrating to all of us to give over five and six minutes to a single story, time during which, many news stories may be reported.

I'm sure all of this is of no solace to you — nor is to us, but I wanted you to know that your are not alone in your thinking.

Sincerely,

Dave Moore

December 31, 1984

Dear Mr. Moore:

As the "most visible" of WCCO's newscasters, permit me, to address this to you; perhaps the station manager should also read it?

If you haven't yet seen it, please note that an article by Dr. Georgette Bennett in the January 5 issue of *TV Guide* says that TV news is typically composed of up to 20% crime content, most of it violent. She claims this is a "public disservice," that it encourages unwarranted fear in the general population, and is an essential distortion of reality. In other words, things are not as bad as they seem, for the average reader. (Thank God if she's right!)

I don't know what the percentage is in the case of WCCO, but since it's our *favorite newscast* we watch it a lot, and in my opinion too, there's way too much emphasis on murder and other assorted violent crime. It's bad enough that these things happen. I don't think they should be publicized at all, much less that they be given as much attention as they are, even by your station.

What do you think? As "Dean of Metro Newspersons," couldn't you exert some of your considerable influence on the "powers that be" to reduce the coverage of violent crime? Many would be grateful for a more upbeat — and realistic — approach, don't you think?

Best wishes for the New Year, in any case.

Sincerely,

Dr. J. H. Foegen

January 9, 1984

Dear Dr. Foegen:

I did not read the TV Guide article, but I would have to suppose the "20% Crime Content Theory" to be correct. In fact, the number may be low.

As it does not in a totalitarian society, crime flourishes in a free or democratic state simply because the consequences are not as severe, and there is a greater chance of acquittal in a court of law.

Thus, in such a society, crime occupying 20% of a half hour news report would not seem out of balance. So I must disagree with you that such reportage is "an essential distortion of reality."

My duties as a newscaster exclude the privilege of exerting influence on the "powers that be," who are the editors of the newscasts and hired, for among their other talents, the skill to rise above "considerable influence."

Which is not to say that I disparage your motive for writing. After all, a concerned citizenry, can give rise to an active citizenry.

Sincerely,

Dave Moore

Dear Mr. Moore,

Next week, February 1-5, all across the nation, Catholic Grade Schools will be celebrating Catholic Schools Week. The theme this year is "The Good News in Education — Catholic Schools."

We at St. Bernard's Grade School will be celebrating with numerous activities — one of which is the release of

31

six-hundred helium balloons at approximately 12 noon on Thursday, Feb. 4th. Inside these balloons are "Good News" messages to our community and people across the nation.

Catholic Schools are "Good News" to students attending them, their parents, their Church, and the communities of which they are a part. Catholic Schools make vital contributions to many people and many institutions in our contemporary world. They are truly "good news" in a multitude of ways, but central to the purpose of Catholic Schools is, of course, another kind of "Good News" — the unique message of hope, trust and love which they share with young people.

Also as part of this week we are asking *you* to share the "good news" of the day on your news program. You are in an influential position and have the power to share the *positive* news. We hear so much negative and depressing news all the time, but you could change that for a few days next week. It would be something different in the news world! Every good reporter strives to have a new slant on a story — surely you can find or challenge your news, weather and sports team to find the "good" in what happens around us in the city and nation.

I suggest five-to-ten minutes of your program could inform listeners of local and national news but you could develop more time to *good news*. Help spread Positive Thinking! February 1-5 is "Good News Week," can you do your part?

Sincerely yours,

Joan Huneke

February 4, 1982

Dear Ms. Huneke,

Your point about "good news" is well made and I admire such a thorough effort to bring home to young people the undeniable fact that life is not all bad.

As you have implied, and as we have learned, the consensus of the populace is that "television newscasts seem to dwell on the bad news." I wonder, in your own words, if the faculty at St. Bernard's might find it fruitful to present this formula to the children:

"The news, as we read it in the newspapers, and hear it on television and radio, means precisely what the word implies: new . . . something new . . . out of the ordinary . . . an event or circumstance that interrupts the flow of normal conditions. Therefore, if most of the news we report is "bad," does it not stand to reason, that normal conditions are positive and bearable and "good?" And shouldn't we rejoice in that?"

In other words, the disquieting and forboding news we hear so often on television is not the dominant force in our lives, but rather is the exceptional force in our lives.

Of course, good, positive news is reported: medical break-throughs, labor contracts resolved, a Bloomington family adopts four Korean orphans, a St.Paul policeman saves the life of an eighty-year-old man, a missing child is found safe etc., etc.

I regret we could not accommodate your wish to devote five to ten minutes to just good news. Such a length of time represents a third of our total news time. News from our local governing bodies must be reported. New parking restrictions must be reported. We must report weather warnings — although I am among those who feel there is much too much of it — and we must report statements of officials that affect our very living.

Again, I certainly am symphathetic to your intent. On the other hand I hope you can appreciate both our limitations and responsibilities and with the philosophy I have advanced, can bring home to young people that the "news" they hear on television and read in the newspapers does not always reflect conditions of misery and despair.

Sincerely,

Dave Moore

PS: Interestingly, our first three stories on 10PM News tonight are: 1) Minneapolis fireman saves child from fire. 2) St.Paul policeman saves the life of an eighty-year-old man.

3) McKnight Foundation makes available a million dollars (each) to Minneapolis and St.Paul to hire four hundred unemployed people in each city.

If the Sevareid "Good News/Bad News" theory is, thus indeed, under question, not so his insightful and eloquent response to the famous speech of Vice President Spiro Agnew in Des Moines, Iowa on November 13, 1969. If memory fails you, Mr. Sevareid's response will indicate the gist of the Vice President's remarks.

**Eric Sevareid Remarks, from Newstape
November 21, 1970:**

The Vice President proposes that network commentators, like this one and brothers Smith and Reynolds down the street at ABC, people of that type, he says, be publicly examined by government personnel. The public has a right to know, he says, our opinions and prejudices. The phrase "people of that type" hurts a bit. We certainly don't think of Mr. Agnew as a type ... we think he's an original. But what really hurts is the thought that maybe nobody has been listening all this time. If, after some thirty years and thousands of broadcasts, hundreds of articles and lectures, and a few books, ones general cast of mind, warts and all, remains a mystery, then we're licked and we fail to see how a few more minutes of examination by government types would solve the supposed riddle. Mr. Agnew wants to know where we stand. We stand, or rather sit, right here in the full glare and the disadvantages against politicians. We can't cast one vote in committee ... an opposite vote on the floor ... can't say one thing in the north and the opposite in the south ... we hold no tenure four years or otherwise, and can be voted out with the twist of the dial. We cannot use invective or epitaphs and cannot even dream of impuning the patriotism of leading citizens ... cannot reduce every complicated issue to yes or no ... black or white ... and would rather go to jail than do bodily injury to the English language. We can't come down on this side or that side of each disputed public issue because we're trying to explain far more than to advocate ... and because some issues don't have two sides ... some have three, four or half a dozen ... and in these matters, we're damned if we know the right answer. This may be why most of us look a bit frazzled while Mr. Agnew looks so serene. Another reason may be that we have to think our own thoughts and write our own phrases. Unlike the Vice President, we don't possess a stable of ghost writers ... come to think of it, if there are mysteries around, unseen spirits motivating the public dialogue, maybe that's the place that could use the glare of public scrutiny ... that stable of anonymity. And finally ... at the risk of sounding a bit stuffy, we might say two things. One ... that nobody in this business expects for a moment that the full truth of anything will be contained in any one account or commentary ... but that through free reporting and discussion, as Mr. Walter Lippman put it ... "the truth will emerge." And second ... that the central point about the free press is not that it be accurate, though it must try to be, not that it even be fair though it must try to be that ... but that it be free. And that means in the first instance, freedom from any and all attempts by the power of government to coerce it or intimidate it or police it in any way.

I think it appropriate to close this section of correspondence with a letter that brings us full-circle to our prefatory comments on "the bad news/good news" syndrome. I am grieved to have misplaced my response. Perhaps there was none. It's possible that I found the writer's thesis so reasoned and well stated as to render me incapable of response. At any rate, while perhaps not undoing altogether the Sevareid theory and my support of it, it certainly indicates that the theory is not, by any means, foolproof.

April 2, 1970

Dear Mr. Moore:

This is a frantic appeal to you and the entire news team whom I believe to be one of, if not, the best in the country. In your respected position as a newscaster and analyzer of that which is newsworthy, I strongly feel that you can help somehow and turn the tide of the mood generated by the news being presented daily.

I will agree 100% that it is not easy to give the news in these troubled times, but a daily dose of nothing but trouble and pessimism is almost too stifling to the majority of the public who knows things aren't all bad, but who could hardly prove it from what they hear and read. We are constantly being informed that only a small segment of our young people are involved in all the violence and destruction that plagues the nation. Yet, who can any longer believe this when so much time and attention is focused on the minority causing it. Every riot from Berkely to Bugwash U. is splashed across our screens and papers and the advocates of such freely babble their vicious attacks on the country and its' system over every mike stuck in their face. The gullibility and naiveté of young people will naturally lead them to join and emulate what appears to them like the "in" thing and one cannot blame them for believing this is the "in" thing, including drugs.

Riots, takeovers, violence and destruction is no longer "news" but a nauseating repeat of a sickness and malignancy that must be stemmed before the scale gets tipped so far in one direction it can never be brought back. One "Tony Dolan" had the guts to stand up and talk back to Abbie Hoffman the other evening on a talk show, but where by all that's holy are all the other Tony Dolans. Someone has got to seek them out, get them on camera and tape, show them to the public and have them castigate and refute the types of Abbie Hoffman. Find that so-called majority and *make* them News. Give us proof they exist for they've been ignored too long. If there is any optimism left anywhere, don't relegate it to a small, insignificant position. Infuse it in every grain of news possible so we may begin to believe that there is a thread of hope left somewhere. What you show and say and do in your position has a great bearing on the attitudes and future actions of your listening public whether you believe it or not and with the great staff you have back you up, you can instill a heap of hope and confidence even while reporting the news "as it is." I can't believe that all news is tragedy and gloom though it certainly appears that way anymore.

Many thanks for reading me out and much luck to you and your group. We listen to you daily and wouldn't turn that knob one more digit for anything.

Sincerely,

Mrs. Gerald Lambert

2

A Member of the Family

If one can luck-it-out long enough in this business, one will develop a stability which, in time, will allow him to become a member of the family. Hundreds of families. Thousands of them, accepting a person whom they have never met, touched, spanked or hugged.

Years ago a seventy-two-year-old lady in Fairmont, Minnesota wrote that since she had recently broken her ankle she could not get into town for the State Fair and would I please "buy (her) a couple of bags of that great salt water taffy that they have down there?" She enclosed a check for two dollars and some odd cents.

I bought the taffy and sent it to her — along with her check. I wrote her "the taffy's on me, my treat."

"Nonsense," she wrote back, "I can pay for my own taffy, thank you!" Enclosed were two one dollar bills.

Unlike so many others, responding to the dozen or so letters that follow, has been easy. To do justice to them, has not.

JULY 1, 1984

DAVE MOORE AND MY FRIENDS AT RADIO STATION WCCO.

ALTHO YOU DO NOT KNOW ME, I THINK OF YOU ALL AS FRIENDS BECAUSE YOU HAVE BEEN COMING INTO MY HOME FOR THESE MANY YEARS WHICH ONLY FRIENDS WOULD DO.

WE RECEIVED A BATTERY POWERED RADIO AS A GIFT
IN 1924 AND THE DIAL HAS BEEN STUCK AT WCCO EVER
SINCE.

MY FAMILY WAS RAISED TO YOUR TIME SIGNALS. MY
HUSBAND WENT TO HIS JOB EVERY DAY ACCORDING TO
YOUR TIME. NOW I LIVE IN A NURSING HOME AND YOUR
STILL WITH ME. I JUST WANT YOU TO KNOW THE JOY AND
HAPPINESS I HAVE RECEIVED FROM YOUR STATION.
WHETHER ITS HOWARD, BOONE AND ERICKSON, BUD OR
CEDRIC, BOB DEHAVEN IN DAYS GONE BY. YOU ARE ALL
MY FRIENDS. KEEP UP THE GOOD WORK.

I SHALL HAVE TO ASK YOU TO PLEASE EXCUSE ER-
RORS. I TYPE THIS WITH ONE FINGER ON MY LEFT HAND.
MY RIGHT SIDE IS PARALIZED FROM STROKES, BUT I
STILL SAY LIFE CAN BE BEAUTIFUL. I HAVE MUCH TO BE
THANKFUL FOR. I STILL HAVE MY MIND AND MY SPEECH
AND HOW THE DAYS JUST FLY BY FOR . THERE ARE
NEVER ENOUGH HOURS IN A DAY FOR ME.

AGAIN I'LL SAY EXCUSE MY TYPING, IM NOT THE
WORLDS GREATEST STENO. KEEP THE LAUGHS AND CHUC-
KLES COMING INTO MY ROOM.

I WANT TO WISH THE BEST OF EVERYTHING TO EACH
AND EVERYONE, MY DEAR FRIENDS AT WCCO.

                              YOUR OLD FRIEND,

                              ARLINE C. ROSINE

                    July 26, 1984

Dear Ms. Rosine,
    *Please do not apologize for your typing; each week I re-
ceive hundreds of well-typed letters that could never make
me feel as happy as your letter has.*
    *Although I work at the television station, I share your
feeling about the folks at radio. I, too, was brought up on
that station. Roger and Steve Cannon and I were at the University together back in the forties and I have known Charlie and Howard Viken for more than twenty-five years.*
    *Can you imagine: as a little boy listening to Bob De-
Haven and Cedric and Clellan Card, and then, as a young*

*man, working alongside them? Tomorrow (the 27th) I will
have been with WCCO for thirty-four years! Has anyone
been luckier?*

*I hope you are very proud: there are few who have
overcome the debilitating effects of a stroke — doesn't
matter if you are not "the world's greatest steno."*

*Thank you for your sweet note. It has made me feel
very good about things.*

Gratefully,

Dave Moore

Jan. 3, 1984

Dear Dave,

I don't feel like a business greeting. You are more like a
friend. Love your news casts. I've tried to write this note
for a long time.

A few weeks ago, you ended your 10 P.M. newscast
with "But nothing for the common cold." Oh, yes there is!
About twenty years ago, when I was a District supervisor
for the *Mpls. Star & Tribune*, I had been calling on my Farm
Service and young carriers all day long. My cold was becoming increasingly worse, tredging in the snow in the
Madison and Dawson areas. At 6 P.M. I drove into Granite
Falls and found Fromm's Drug Store still open. I walked in
and asked Carl Fromm if he could give me anything for my
cold so I could play my duplicate bridge. He reached on the
shelf and said, "Here's something new." I swallowed one
capsule right there; even without water. On my way to my
duplicate partner, I stopped to call on my Farm Service
Salesman. His wife, a former student of mine, invited me to
have dinner with them. I answered, "Oh, thank you — but
I have such a cold." I though a moment — "Oh, it's done!
It's gone!" Chexit — what a miracle! I enjoyed a delicious
dinner, played a good game of bridge and even won a mas-
ter point that night.

I have never had a cold for all these years. Always have
a Chexit in my purse. *Occasionally*, if I feel a sniffle coming

on as in church with the door opening a lot and there's a draft, I'll break off a half one, and it's over. I seldom take any, I'm really immune to colds!

I'll grant, it doesn't help everyone, but for me it is great, and at seventy-seven I don't want a cold.

This is too long, I could have told it in twenty words, maybe.

Sincerely,

Gladys Golie

Gladys Golie

P.S. I was a fond listener of Cedric Adams' newscasts, & knew him personally since we both worked for the *Star & Tribune*. Yours is even better.

January 10, 1984

Dear Ms. Golie,

Thank you for your cheery letter. How I cherish it! Such a refreshing departure from the run of correspondence that list the annoyances and difficulties of contemporary living.

The enjoyment of continued living has been brought to life for me by your letter: the simple expedient of dissolving a cold, the evoking of the ambience of the small town drug store and the assured wisdom of its proprietor.

I should some day like to visit Fromm's Drug Store and visit with Carl.

Farm service salesmen, a splendid dinner and a good game of bridge are all sources of basic enjoyment that so many of us have allowed to elude us.

And as for the Chexit: I passed the sample you enclosed to my twenty-two-year-old son, Alex, who, like you, a few hours later, proclaimed it a miracle!

He thanks you and I especially thank you for brightening my day.

Gratefully,

Dave Moore

September 16, 1985

Dear Mr. Moore,

    I just thought I would write you, buster, and let you know about the trouble you are causing in my household. Ever since the word about you leaving the 10 p.m. report got out, I've been having trouble with my twenty-seven-year-old wife, Teresa Rico.

    Now this next part gets a little embarassing, but here it is. Each time she sees you on the news, or views the promo for your retrospective, she begins bellyaching. Actually, she begins moaning. "Ooohhhh, my honey, my honey," she says. "What am I going to do?" I know. I know. But that's what she says. I don't dislike you, Mr. Moore, and have great respect for you as a newsman, but I have taken to informing her that "He just reads the news, he's only one part of the broadcast; besides, you'll still see him on the 6 p.m. show." It doesn't work. "My honey's leaving me," she says "and it just won't be the same."

    So I asked her, point blank, "How long has this been going on?" Now this next part is a little hard to believe, but here it is. "Since Ground Hog's Day a few years back," she says. Go figure it. She says you concluded a 10 p.m. show with your observances on how stupid Ground Hog's Day is, and that did it for her.

    Anyway, when she watches the news these days, she takes special delight in your offhand remarks and irreverent comments. "Ooohhh, my honey," she says. "What am I going to do?" So, there you have it. I'd appreciate it, fella, if you could drop her a line, breaking this thing off once and for all, for my sake. Tell her someone writes all your material, even your clever remarks, and that you are just a witless dolt, or something to that effect. It may save our marriage.

Good Riddance, Sort of,

Barry J. Johnson

P.S. Just between you and me, I'll miss you too.

41

October 1, 1985

Dear Mr. Johnson,

Sympathetic though I am, I am not sure I have the necessary skills to assist you in what appears to be a near insoluble problem.

From what I can glean from your letter, what we have here is a twenty-seven-year-old woman with the wondrously eclectic name of Teresa Rico Johnson (!), who has developed an affinity to a sixty-one-year-old news-reading television image as well as an antipathy toward ground hogs, the curious nature of which is such that the mere scandalzing of the little creeps sends her into spasms of joy and cries of, "Oh, my honey!!"

She thus seems eminently qualified to be soul-mate to a "witless dolt."

Perhaps on the occasion of my next 6 o'clock television appearance she could leave a little something out for me, on a plate, like some cheese or bacon, as a means of testing her fidelity.

Meantime I suggest you begin looking into the complications so often attendant to the filing of commitment papers.

Dave Moore

Another in the same vein, but fifteen years earlier. This in response to my decision to put the Sealy Saturday Night Bedtime News to bed for good. After nine years of exhausting Saturdays the program was losing its allure for me. Although the program was a pretty well kept secret in the first two or three years, as I look back on it it was a program of self-fulfillment. For several reasons: It was a marvelous opportunity to put into practice the art of concise writing and meticulous production; I was left to my own devices, despite occasional moments of questionable taste and artistic decorum; As a succinct roundup of the major news and sporting events of the day, I did manage to get it all in, and not always irreverently, whimsically, or satirically. And of course, not unlike stealing from the cookie jar, it was fun to play the authoritarian at ten o'clock each Saturday, and two or three hours later become the buffoon. But most rewarding of all, absolutely thrilling to me was how everyone on the Saturday night staff pitched in, in thousands of ways to make the program work — a genuine, honest-to-goodness team effort, without which there'd have been no Bedtime Newₜs.

I have, sorrowfully, misplaced my response to the letter that follows.

December 28, 1970

Dear Dave,

My husband has known about us for many years. My daughter was aware of our weekly trysts and understood. Was it something I said or did or intimated or implied that has made you decide to break things off?

I've tried not to be possessive. I haven't minded sharing you with your wife and thousands of others. I didn't make a scene when you took occasional vacations and were temporarily out of my life.

It wasn't easy to watch Channel 4 news programs on evenings you were not working, but I managed. It was almost unbearable watching the Bedtime Nooz when you were on vacation, but I bravely bit my lip and consoled myself with the thought that you would soon return. There have been Saturdays I have stayed up only to watch you — and then been informed that, due to special programming that caused regular broadcasting to continue later than usual, the Bedtime Nooz would not be on that night. I've even managed to survive that.

Now the Sunday paper tells me you're giving up our Saturday nights in March. I don't want to make a scene. I've made every effort not to cry or become hysterical. I wish I could smile bravely and say, "Okay, it was fine while it lasted. Let's part as friends." But I can't bring myself to be so noble!

If the station wants to end this affair, I'll send petitions. If Sealy wants to drop its sponsorship, I'll find you a new sponsor. If your wife wants to spend more time with you, I'll beg her to change her mind and let you out that night.

Please, please don't take away my Twin You's, my evenings with Visiting Mattress Dealers, my watching you watch TV on my TV. Don't take away that scoreboard and the flashes of incorrect personages behind you!

Oh, White Knight, say it isn't so!

Hopefully,

Irene Peltz

(Mrs.) Irene Peltz

August 18, 1970

Dear Dave:

We just saw The Bedtime Newz and it immediately was voted the most refreshing information (?) program of the decade. I'm sorry now that you trapped me into those nose-holding statements. My veracity is now in question.

Further, Charles Kuralt was at the viewing, and he sang your praises for the nightly news presentation. I'm pleased to be in such company.

Come back and see us when we both have time to lift a few.

All the best,

Walt

Walter Cronkite

As a well-meaning friend once said to me, "When you grow up in a place the memories become indelibilized in your mind." (This is the same gentleman, who, years earlier, had said, "The trouble with your job is everyone knows you; you have no privacy. I'd rather be synonymous.")

Generally, the life of a television newscaster is a nomadic one. He or she becomes transient not always by choice, but rather by plummeting ratings, obstreperous managers and editors, imperfect geography, or serf-like wages.

Rare, I think, is the newscaster privileged to work on native ground. I've loved it! It has kept me in touch with old, old friends, who would have been long lost friends had they not known where to reach me. It has provided me with a natural assurance and confidence on such occasions as election night and Svenskarnaas Dag. These idiocyncracies of time and place are the kinds of things that the non-native newscasters must learn as they go.

As a captive of nostalgia, and, occasionally, melancholia, I am pleased when the *Minneapolis Star and Tribune* or *City Pages* or *The Reader* asks me to supply them with a memory of growing up in Minneapolis. The following is a loving remembrance of a woodworking teacher, and the response from the man's brother.

Minneapolis Star & Tribune
May 21, 1985:

Making the move from grade school to junior high school can be a very nervous experience for a twelve-year-old lacking confidence and intellectual potential.

My anxieties were eased not at all by the prospect of the "shop class" requirements — Electricity, Sheet Metal, Printing, and most frightening of all, Woodwork. To this day, my sense and feeling for things technical are just a cut below that of a three year old — giving myself the benefit of the doubt.

Fully aware that Woodworking class lay ahead, I trembled the entire summer vacation preceding the opening of fall classes and the 7th grade at Ramsey Junior High School. But the day arrived and there I was in the class of Mr. Walter Machula, a mountainous man with a booming, wall-shattering bass voice who was said to have idolized Captain Bligh as a disciplinarian.

For the first day of orientation, Mr. Machula, in a no-nonsense manner that was not at all comforting to me, informed the class of the five woodworking (FIVE!) projects we would make; beginning with Ash Tray, followed by Book Ends, Picture Frame, Pen and Pencil Holder, and concluding with Magazine Rack. He displayed each of these items as they had been turned out by a past class. They were the most wondrous wood creations I had ever seen!

Suffice it to say that the troubles I encountered were even more terrifying than my fearful heart had anticipated.

While most of the class was quickly dispensing with the first two projects, I was still struggling with Ash Tray.

Mr. Machula, despite his forboding bearing, and despite what I had heard of him, proved a man of infinite patience and genuine compassion. For when I, at long last, timidly presented the finished project to him, he surveyed it quizzically and said, "Well, David, as an Ash Tray I'm afraid this is "Fail" work. I tell you what we'll do: I'll give you a "D" and we'll call it a Paper Weight."

That beautiful man, Walter Machula, taught me that there is more than one way of looking at something.

Including himself.

6/20/85

Dear Mr. Moore,

It was with pleasure & a deep feeling of pride & remembrance that we read the article you wrote in the *Mpls. Star & Tribune* of May 21 about the influence of Walter Machula on your adult life.

Walter was the oldest brother in our family & we always respected his opinions & advice so it has pleased us very much to know that he had a good influence on the life of such a *well known & well liked* person as you are. Many friends & other relatives have seen the article & talked to us about it, all of which has made us relive many memories.

Walter passed away in 1966, his wife also a few years later, but he has a daughter & grandchildren living in St. Paul.

Thank you for the memories!

Alfred Machula (youngest brother)
Alfred Machula
(youngest brother)

June 25, 1985

Dear Mr. Machula,
Thank you for your kindly note.
I knew your brother had passed away but somehow I thought it more recently than 1966.
He was truly a dear fellow. On occasion when the Appollo Club (Note: Mr. Machula sang in the Appollo Club) appeared at Northrup Auditorium, or even here at the station, I would introduce myself to him and he seemed to enjoy the remembrance.
I think your brother favored me because even though I was certainly not a good student and showed no potential for becoming one, he knew I was doing my best and trying hard.
I'm sure it is comforting for you to know I have heard from other Ramsey grads about the article, and they all agreed.

Dave Moore

_____

December 04, 1984

Dear Dave:
I am writing you this letter in nostalgia in reference to the book by Benedict E. Hardman, "Everybody Called Him Cedric," and I know you know who Cedric Adams was.
Before you retire or die, God forbid, I wish you and WCCO would do a documentary on Cedric as there are a lot of the old timers around that tuned him in at 10:00 P.M. for the news and bought a lot of Holseum bread.
Cedric did the talent shows for Phillip's 66 at a lot of little old home town schools, mine included, and then did the news live via phone — Boy, has the media changed.
Well, Dave, just food for thought if you would like to do something different, because there are more old timers out there than you might think and being it is WCCO's big

birthday year, give it a try. I don't claim any royalties, just that he was one hell of a guy.

Sincerely,

Carlton D. Lohse

December 7, 1984

Dear Mr. Lohse,

Thank you for the good idea.

You can imagine how I felt to be working with Cedric. From the time I was old enough to even perceive the radio, Cedric was a part of my life — at the family dinner table and from my own desk radio in my bedroom — Cedric was a part of my every day.

And there, fifteen years later or so, I was working with him! And Clellan Card! And Toby Print! And John Ford!

I'll put your idea forth to our assignment people, but I'm afraid it will fall on deaf ears. You had to know him and remember him to appreciate him — and very few of them, if any, do.

Dave Moore

Dear Sir!

When I listen on WCCO evening news I see some one who is different from the other newscasters. The same movements, the same smile and the same voice. Many years ago, lets say forty-five or fifty, the three of us met at the Universities Farms Bee Yard. Reinhart, Dave Moore and I. I am sure Dave that you were the first person to take live movies of the Bees in Minnesota. Reinhart took notes while I opened the bee hive, took out frames with bees. You took pictures to show people that they can work with bees with out getting stung.

You Dave also wanted to take pictures of the queen and poor me I had to take out three or four frames to find her. None of us got stung! Dave do you remember that event?

For twenty or more years I put bee demonstrations at the Minnesota State Fair and I am sure that you took pictures of me in the Bee Cage. Those were the happy days of my life. Let me tell you Dave that I am the oldest Apiary inspector in Minnesota alive.

All my chiefs from Blaker to Floyd are gone where there is no return. Four of them. You do remember Dr. Tanguary, Dr. Hydak, Father Yager, they are gone. and Prof. Rugles. I also had three deputies and they are gone. I feel like that old oak tree on the prairie who have survived all the storms.

Dave, I am ninety-five years old. Please add six months more. When I watch the news on WCCO I see you Dave. Then the memories of old come back to me.

Pardon me for telling you all these!

Good luck Dave, I will be watching you on W.C.C.O.

Sincerely,

Almar.

Almar Alsen

P.S. — Say Hello to Bud Kraeling he has that old sweet smile even when he tells me watch out for Tornado or thirty below zero. Smile Bud Smile, and the world will smile with you!

EDITOR'S NOTE: Mr. Alsen informs us that he has turned ninety-nine this year.

February 3, 1984

Dear Mr. Alsen,

Thank you for such a wonderful letter!

You have recalled such a marvelous time, in such a fine, descriptive way, I have entertained the idea of saying, Yes, I am that Dave Moore." But alas, Mr. Alsen, I cannot.

You see, forty-five years ago I'd have been just four-teen years old.

I'm sure that as a youngster, I may have seen you in action at the State Fair.

I shall treasure your letter as the remnant of a good life lived.

Please continue in good health.

Dave Moore

November 17, 1970

Dear Mr. Moore,

I have just listened to your program on trains.

Forty years ago we took the Northfield & Southern railway from Orchard Gardens to Mpls. Many of our neighbors commuted daily to down town. The track still lies there. No one sees a train on those tracks very often. Isn't it sad that these facilities can not be made available to the riding public? Think of the polution it would avoid in this area.

Three years ago, my husband and I took our eighteen-year-old daughter to the west coast. It cost us only $30.00 less than flying. We wanted our daughter to see the countryside & to realize that speed does not compensate for all things. How ever, as you brought out to-nite, the service was abominable, we were cold & had to use blankets, which we had sense enough to bring. No one bothered to do anything to make the trip enjoyable. If just half were done, such as airlines do, I'm sure many people would ride trains & enjoy it. It would take the older drivers off the free-ways.

Just as death & taxes are inevitable, so will we all grow older & be a menace to others. Trains could have the facilities for traveling young parents. Why not hotels and facilities to attract people who might like to tour the lovely towns by local busses? It seems to me there is an untapped source of revenue in these ideas. We are being pushed into

50

automobiles or jets, which we do not want, regardless of what the automobile industry & highway engineers say.

I thank you if you have read all this!

Sincerely,

Mrs. F.O. Zimmerman

Mrs. F.O. Zimmerman

November 20, 1970

Dear Mrs. Zimmerman,

Thank you for your most illuminating and perceptive thoughts. You have touched upon some points that evaded us altogether and I am sorry we failed to think of them ourselves. Or perhaps, on second thought, it may have occurred to us, but fifteen minutes is such a terribly short time to include all of the arguments for rail passenger travel.

For instance, as I read your letter, I thought, "Why, of course! What better education could a young person receive than by train travel — through the small hamlets of the country, getting a first hand look at the contrasting physical elements of one state to another!"

We have been delighted by the public response to the program. We hope it will help to produce a positive effect.

Gratefully,

Dave Moore

November 15, 1983

Dave:

To refresh your memory, I ran into you on Monday November 14th outside of B. Dalton's on the Mall. We discussed your interview with Dick Pomerantz.

Let me say it was a pleasure talking to you. Since moving to the Twin Cities in 1976 I've been impressed with your presentation of the news, as well as the personality you project on specials. To be honest, I thoroughly enjoyed and miss your "Moore on Sunday Program."

I admired your humbleness in saying you don't know why anyone would want to interview you as your convictions aren't what they may have been several years ago. Keep in mind I think you'd be surprised the soft yet powerful impact you have on people. I've felt it, enjoyed it & thank you for it.

Best Always

Lawrence A. Ellis

Lawrence A. Ellis

November 22, 1983

Dear Mr. Ellis:

Thank you for your kindly note.

I enjoyed meeting you that day; I certainly must have because I don't think I've admitted to anyone that I have no convictions. It was strange to hear me say that.

And not out of "humbleness" as you have suggested, but more out of fear and bewilderment.

I suppose, as times change, convictions, once firm, take on an elusive quality — unless, that is, we are willing to change. Change has never come easy to me.

On the other point you are probably correct: I do seem to have an impact on people. I wish to hell I didn't. I think it comes from being a presence in homes for so many years — like a chair, or a painting.

At any rate I appreciate your thoughtfulness in taking the time to write. I hope we might meet again.

Dave Moore

I list the following letter among my favorites. I addressed my reply to: Edward Johnson, "Bachelor's Paradise."

Dec 22-85

Mr. Dave Moore,

I am seventy-two years old last July 14. I've watched & listened to you for as long as I can remember. I'm writing to say thank you for all the wonderful hours I've had watching you, and when there were two of you Dave's talking like you were different people.

I've often wished I could have been on TV on newstime with you. How honored I'd have been.

So my friend you & your family keep well, & happy and your crew. I love you all, I shall keep praying for hurting people & all of you, God Bless you all

Edward A.R. Johnson

Edward A.R. Johnson
"Bachelors Paradise"

I have been single twenty-five years But I love dancing & go to Belroy often. Id like to meet you there ???

January 10, 1986

Dear Mr. Johnson,

What a treat to hear from you! It's people like you I love hearing from: folks who've been around and probably "through" a lot more than most of us, but are enjoying the most out of every minute of life.

Dancing! Dancing! You're doing at seventy-two what I gave up at twenty-two! I always did well at dancing until they started the music.

Those old commercials (where there were two of me) were Sealy Posturepedic spots that I wrote for the old

Saturday night Bedtime Newʒs, from November '62 to March 13, 1971.

I am honored and flattered that you have remembered them.

I wish you well in your "Bachelor's Paradise."

Dave Moore

Feb 6, 1986

Dear Dave Moore:-

When I saw you receive your Dupont-Columbia award last evening I was so happy for you and proud of you. That you had received two other ones really tells the tale.

My husband received his Ph.D. many, many years ago from Columbia. When I saw the library during the ceremony it took me back to the spring of 1930 when we with hundreds of others filled the steps for the Easter Sunrise service. Such lovely music, an awing experience, and a special memory.

Best of everything to you from an eighty-nine-year-old admirer.

Very sincerely,

Pauline S. Meredith
(Mrs. W.F.)

February 10, 1986

Dear Mrs. Meredith,

Thank you for sharing your memory of Columbia University.

It was my second trip there and I must say that upon entering the impressive gates across 116th Street I felt the same tingling sensation that I remember from the first time five years ago.

The august ambience of the pillared buildings, partic-
ularly at night, is enthralling!

I have always associated Columbia with Nicolas Mur-
ray Butler, the Hall of Fame, Dwight Eisenhower and Lou
Little and his surprising Rose Bowl football team of
1933 (?). But once inside the gates, it is far more than any
of that.

Again, thank you. I have many friends at Gustavus
Adolphus and it's always pleasing to hear from someone at
St. Peter.

Dave Moore

Dear Dave Moore,

Meant to drop you a line after my visit to Chicago last
summer. Was so sure I would hear some broadcasting that
would be outstanding. Nothing even equalled W.C.C.O.

My day begins and ends with W.C.C.O.

Twas nice to see Ron Majors I believe on W.M.A.Q. Chicago was my home for many years.

Listened to your broadcast tonite on The I Team and the
right to privacy. It took me back a number of years. My
husband was thrown out of the Hudson ambulance en-
route to Vets Hospital. The driver ran the light.

He was taken to Anchor where he was treated.

They put stitches in his scalp wrapped an Ace bandage
around his head. He was quite a rotund man.

He stood stripped to the waist with a lock of hair stick-
ing up thru the bandage, when the reporters walked in and
said, "How about a picture." The poor man was in shock he
had seven broken ribs. Of course he didn't object.

At six o'clock my husband's picture was on the air. I
was so embarrassed. Had I been there, I fear their cameras
would have rolled if not their heads. I am not a violent
woman and am only five feet tall but I could have never
coped with that.

That is many years ago but I'll never forget it. Believe
me I *know* what an invasion of privacy is and bad taste

thrown in. I am sure they were from the Dispatch.

You can be rightfully proud of your W.C.C.O. crew.

Sincerely,

Floy Johnson

Floy Johnson

April 11, 1984

Dear Ms. Johnson,

On the very day your letter arrived I fulfilled a scheduled speaking engagement to a group of First National Bank of Minneapolis employees.

Since much of the question and answer period following my remarks concerned the subject of "invasion of privacy," I took the liberty of reading your letter to the group, although I did not use your name.

It added credence to my argument that more often than not, we are indeed guilty of invading the privacy of others.

I thank you for taking the time to share your experience and I do hope you are not upset by my sharing your thoughtful letter with others.

Sincerely,

Dave Moore

June 1, 1986

Dear Mr. Moore:

Very often I have wondered why WCCO does not bring back the "Weather Window" of the '50s. It was fun writing to our relatives and friends and saying, "Be sure to watch WCCO on Wednesday noon — I'll be waving to you."

Also, I remember being part of the audience for the 10 p.m. news. It was exciting watching you people present the news and watching the camera people, besides (again) waving to Mom and Dad, etc. "at home."

Your station used to be so folksy. You have terrific personnel (better than the other stations), however, I find myself tempted to watch Channel 5 more just because they show other places and people now. They've "lightened up" for the summer and I wish WCCO would do the same thing. I never like to criticize unless I can also offer a solution, and I'm not the only one who misses the above two things your channel had to offer.

So glad Pat is back! People who have bumped into her have said she is so pleasant and nice, besides being so pretty and doing a bang-up job. And glad you haven't entirely quit. Keep up the good work WCCO!

Sincerely,

Lorraine Cisewski

June 16, 1986

Dear Ms. Cisewski,

Thank you for your kind thoughts. Your letter took me back many, many years ago to the old "Weather Window" on 9th Street. It attracted many people and it was a particularly pleasant gathering place at night for the people who lived downtown. In my evening strolls to Walgreens, I came to know many of them quite well.

Your letter also brings up an interesting point: folksiness. As you have pointed out "Channel 5 has lightened up for the summer... getting out to show other places and people." Channel 11, I might add, has started to follow suit.

I'm not sure it's quite the appropriate thing to do on a daily newscast, when time to report the news of the day is so limited. Frankly, I question the motives of those two channels. I wonder if it isn't a not-so-subtle attempt to win viewers. Why, of a sudden, are they doing this when it hasn't been done for years?

It is necessary? Certainly our local newscasts do get around to the various communities to report the news in those areas, and in so doing, present many of the views of the people in those communities.

I tend to agree with what Joe Soucheray wrote recently in his column in the St.Paul Pioneer Press: He questions whether television news departments — as well as newspapers — should be chummy with their viewers and subscribers. That "chuminess...is a contrived distraction...that distorts the purpose of delivering news in the first place, which is to provide as much information as possible that affects a person's life."

I can certainly see your point. There is something to be said for friendliness. On the other hand, I wonder if you can't see the danger inherent in such a practice: to guarantee an audience of not only those people who have waved on television, but also their friends, and neighbors and relatives.

Would we not, then, be guilty of acquiring an audience by affection instead of by earning their trust? I think affection will come if we do our jobs properly, keeping our audience up to date, day by day.

But again, I thank you for taking the time to write. Your letter certainly set me to thinking.

Dave Moore

February 5th, 1986

Dear Mr. Moore,

We need your help. A friend of ours named Joe Nolan (no relation to the Orioles' catcher,) refuses to attend a baseball game at the dome. He won't let us drag him to a game until he has proof that Dave Moore has been to a baseball game in there. Now we've seen you do reports from inside the dome, but Joe maintains that you, the purist, leave before the ballgame starts.

He is a big baseball fan and Twins fan, but he insists that until YOU go, HE won't. He even had a recurring nightmare last summer that he was standing outside the Hump, being offered free All-Star Game tickets and after turning them down, saw you accept the same offer and go in.

We share your love of the game and your extreme distaste for indoor baseball and baseball on carpets, but we feel that dome ball is better than no ball (except for the occasional drive to Milwaukee or Chicago, or visits to relatives in Boston, Baltimore and Los Angeles.)

So we need to know whether or not you've been to a ballgame in the dome. If you could spare a minute to dash off a note or make a phone call to him to settle this matter, we would be eternally grateful.

Thanks very much for listening.

Sincerely,

Dave Draeger
Denny Dore

February 10, 1986

Gentlemen:

I must say, I certainly admire the lengths to which friends would go to persuade anyone into that...that place.

I am sorry I cannot be of some service to you in your mission. You'll have to accomplish it on your own.

For the record, I have been in that...that place three times: twice on assignment, and once to play in a charity softball game.

On all three occasions I became nauseous.

On one of the assignments I left immediately upon completion of the work. On the other I stayed for nearly two innings, leaving just after Gary Gaetti tripped and fell fielding a swinging bunt from Julio Franco.

Also for the record: I do not — repeat — do not disparage others from that place. In fact I envy them their objectivity.

My personal abhorrence is a mere exercise in health preservation.

Dave Moore

When one makes a late and superficial entry as a "member of the family" as I have, one must be aware that there are boundaries, even in the most familial of families. I offer the following true story as a demonstration of the economic aspect of those boundaries.

Grocery Store

It was a soft evening in April. 1959? 1960? (How dates decay and fall away in the used mind!)

After folding up the Ten O'Clock News and leaving the television station I was perilously close to home and had not yet cashed my check to get money for the childrens' school savings account the next day.

Ah, here! I'll stop here. What told me it was a little "Mom and Pop" grocery was the jangling of the bells when I opened the door, and before I could close it there appeared from behind the cash register a fragile little man in his seventies sent over by Central Casting to play the role of Pop.

A cheery little voice. "Yes sir, may I help...Oh, my gosh! Oh, my Heavens!!"

Groping his way around the cash register he came to a halt, steadying himself against the register. There he stood, staring, transfixed. I thought I caught an eye trembling. To the sudden interloper it must have seemed an odd tableau, for I stood similarly transfixed. Transfixed by his transfixation. Although I had been reading the nightly news on television for a year or two, I was not the Dave Moore as we have come to know him — warm, compassionate, trusted, and now, avuncular — and was thus unprepared to grasp what was to become a common occurrence in years to come.

I terminated the interminable silence with, "Are you alright, sir?"

"Yes, yes! Oh my, yes! You aren't...are you the...is it possible that. Aren't you the man who reads the news to us?"

"Yes," I said, "I believe I am."

"Oh, my Heavens! You are ...?"

"Dave Moore." Why have I always been uncomfortable saying my name?

"Yes, yes! Davemoore, Davemoore, Oh my, Heavens!!"

A step backward.

"Rosalie! Rosalie! Come here! Quick!"

As he called out, his gaze remained riveted on me. What to do with my hands? Through an opening in the wall behind him appeared a squat little lady — she, too, from Central Casting — her hair in a bun atop her head, her hands twisting in the apron that hung from an ample mid-section. Myopic beyond patience of even the most sympathetic eye-chart, she squinted first at Pop, then at me.

Gently nudging her closer to me, Pop asked, "Do you know who this is? Do you?"

Haven't the foggiest," she said.

"This is Dave Moore!" The name came out as a drum-roll. She suddenly seemed alive. "The man who reads the news on TV?"

"Yes, Maam. Dave Moore! The man who reads the news on TV!"

"Well, I'll be!"

"Yup. Dave Moore. Right here in our store! Just think!!"

Then Mom "I'll be'ed" again. Pop "I'll be'ed again. We all "I'll be'ed" together and Pop found the composure he needed to ask, "Well, Dave Moore, what can we do for you?"

"I want to buy some things," I said, "Some milk, some bread. But first I need to know if you can cash a check."

"Why sure," he said, "Do you have any identification?"

3

The Taking of Umbrage, the Venting of Spleen, the Incurring of Wrath

In this section, we shall deal with the many ways in which the television newscaster, either by design, innocence, or faulty judgement manages to attack the vulnerabilities of his audience, who, in turn, will counter attack.

"The Nature Of The Beast" is what we call this syndrome we use to rationalize most of our indiscretions, and is peculiar to broadcast journalism as opposed to the print medium.

It may be achieved by (1) a raised or lowered eyebrow, (2) a questionable or sudden change in tonal inflection, (3) an unwise choice of words, (4) an unfortunate juxtaposition of words producing, often times, a wicked double entendre, (5) a grammatical or factual error which the newscaster might have found had he carefully checked his script before air time, (6) losing his place in the script or on the Teleprompter, (7) misreading the script or Teleprompter, or (8) suppressing a burp.

The newscaster notwithstanding, there are self-contained pitfalls within the Beast itself. The Beast does not, for example, inspire rapt attention from its audience. Anything can happen at any moment; (1) the telephone may ring on a critical word, (2) the viewer may be listening from the kitchen as he searches the refrigerator for the mayonnaise, (3) someone may suddenly engage the viewer in conversation, or (4) the viewer may be busy injuring someone in the room.

In other words, the television newscaster and the viewer can be victims of Distraction, and the essence of what is reported is either distorted or lost altogether.

Or, in other instances the newscaster may jangle the viewer's nervous system by means of the dangerous ad-lib — the cute, smarty-pants improvisation that occasionally erupts from all of us who are cursed with delusions of comic genius.

And what is the poor viewer's recourse? Generally speaking, letters of storm and rage did not reach quantitative heights until the late sixties when the traditional — yes, rather staid — news format was abandoned for what has become the "team" or "gang" or "happy talk" approach.

Until 1966, or thereabouts, the half-hour "news block" contained three independent information entities: fifteen minutes of news, five minutes of weather, ten minutes of sports news, each entity isolated from the other by commercials and station "breaks." For all the audience knew, each presenter may have been working in different studios, each responsible for the activity in his own bailiwick, thus precluding verbal, personal contact between the three.

Enter, in the late sixties, the "just plain folks" approach: a not very subtle means of playing on the viewers' susceptibility to the virtues of hearth, home and family. There we are, sitting up there, chatting back and forth just like real folk exchanging small talk in a free flow of idle banter and mindless chit-chat, off-setting our positions as messengers of doom. Meanwhile, this very format of togetherness, provides an inescapable transitionary devise, enabling us to move from one segment of the newscast to the other — news to weather, weather back to news, news to sports, sports back to news — to bring a continuity of ease and friendliness to the proceedings. But it also opens the way for unthinking, potentially offensive remarks that rouse the righteous indignation of an otherwise calm and peaceable people. The format, for good or ill, has become the staple of television newscasts across the country.

Let us proceed with a letter from a lady who took offense by my recall of a famous cartoon in which we see a little boy glaring at his plate on the table and saying, "I say it's spinach and I say to hell with it." The comment followed a report by Marcia Fleur who had interviewed young people about their most "unfavorite" traditional Thanksgiving dishes.

Dec. 3, 1985

Dear Staff Members of WCCO-TV News,

I am writing to express my disappointment and dismay with two parts of WCCO-TV's evening news with Dave Moore on Channel 4 of November 28, 1985 — Thanksgiving.

One portion included interviews of students at a Columbia Heights school, with the interviewer asking the students what they did not like about Thanksgiving dinner. I myself enjoyed a big dinner that day, but did *you* consider how a viewer who was *hungry* that evening felt when he or she heard students talk about perfectly good food as "gross?" Parents that I know want their children to be appreciative and thankful, and do not need your reporters seeking and promoting and chuckling at such ingratitude as shown on this newscast. This was especially appalling on a day when we need to thank God for the blessings we enjoy.

Then Dave Moore added a comment about spinach and said, "to *hell* with it." Mr. Moore, hell is a real place, and you should not include the word in jokes, and you certainly should not use such vile language during a newscast.

Our family watches television on a very restricted schedule. In the future our restrictions will include newscasts on your station.

Sincerely,

Connie M. Pearson

Connie M. Pearson

December 12, 1985

Dear Ms. Pearson,

Your letter of December 3rd has troubled me, hence my delay in responding. You are certainly deserving of a re-

sonsible reply, but I am not so sure that your point (s) is (are) well taken.

Childhood and early adolescence abhorrence of certain foods on the table — even the Thanksgiving table — is well known. Like puberty and pimples it is one of the idio-syncracies of growing up, acknowledged and accepted by child guidance professionals and tolerant parents.

Given that, and in the un-thinking world of the adolescent, I don't feel Marcia Fleur's report reflected a young person's "ingratitude." Nor does it disparage the unfortunate circumstances of the "viewer who was hungry." At some time in his or her life I'm sure there were foods that were repugnant to <u>them</u>.

In your childhood, Ms. Pearson, was there not a serving of rutabaga, creamed onions or candied yams that you found "gross?"

I thought I was on fairly safe ground footnoting the story with the famous cartoon devised by the esteemed James Thurber and E.B. White. On the occasion of Mr. White's recent death, it was affectionately recalled by many respectable publications. Over the years it has appeared in national dietary journals, on bulletin boards of home economics classes and in books by famous chefs and food critics. It may, in fact, be one of the most widely reproduced and oft-quoted of all cartoons, simply because it embraces a condition more than casually familiar to each of us.

On the other hand, your empathy with the less fortunate is to be commended, and I am genuinely sorry that the entire episode offended your sensibilities.

Dave Moore

December 16, 1985

Dear Mr. Moore:

I resented your crack on the 6 PM Report tonight, describing historic preservationists as "sentimentalists." The inference is very clear, and very derogatory, not to say insulting.

I want the city to save the State Theater because I care about the visual and cultural quality of downtown Minneapolis. I presume you care about such things as well, so please choose your words with more care — many viewers probably had their stereotypical notion of the Preservationist confirmed by Dave Moore tonight.

Occasionally, your flippancy and good humor on the air can cause some unintentional damage. This is such a case, especially when City Council members are making their final decisions on the State's future.

In many ways, Hennepin Avenue and Minneapolis as a whole will be less interesting if the State goes down. It's just one building, but it represents a period in the city's history which has been entirely destroyed by insensitive developers and disinterested civic leaders.

The public needs to know that it isn't sentimentalism but *sensitivity* to the city's history and architectural splendor which is motivating the effort to save the State. Broadcasters like yourself can inform the public or you can simply confirm existing stereotypes.

Every word counts, Dave.

By the way, you're a great broadcaster.

Sincerely,

Jay Furst

December 20, 1985

Dear Mr. Furst,

Since when is a "sentamentalist" an "insulting" word? By what authority is it "derogatory?"

It was not broadcast as a "crack." Nor was it delivered with "flippancy" or an attempt at "good humor." The word was "chosen with care" and articulated with pride — in a headline — because I am a "sentimentalist," and so, too are you. Pray, what distinguishes the "preservationist" from the "sentimentalist?" In my view they are synonymous terms. How elitist of you to even assume that "viewers have stereotypical notion(s) of the Preservationist!"

And please, spare me the lectures about the State Theatre. I worked three years there in the early forties as an usher, and on more than one occasion have publicly indicated that no one wants the edifice preserved more than I.

Furthermore, beyond the bounds of ethics and proper journalism behavior, I have, time and again, used innuendo and cheap shot to disparage the destruction of, to name only a few, the Curtis Hotel, Charlie's, Davies Mortuary, and, most vociferously of all, the laying to waste of Metropolitan Stadium, which took from us not only one of the finest sports arenas in the country, but put away, beyond retrieval, a special ambience never to be duplicated by that abomination, the symbol of industrial greed, The Metrodome.

And finally, I am not a "great broadcaster" and I resent your saying so. Edwin C. Hill, Elmer Davis and Lowell Thomas were "great broadcasters." From the aforementioned admissions it is obvious I do not belong in their class.

After all that, I wish you a Happy New Year.

Dave Moore

P.S. Please forgive the typos. This was written in rage.

One of the low points in my life — and there have been very few — occurred in September, 1981 when I was arrested for driving while under the influence. The newspapers in both cities made note of the event and I feared an onslaught of poisonous mail. There was but one such letter.

1/16/82

Dear Mr. Moore:
    I assume you have read one of the enclosed clippings,
perhaps both. You've been given another break (or did you
pay for it?). I hope you take the opportunity to get well
this time. Next time may be too late for you and someone
else.

                Sincerely,

                Bob Pendleton

                Bob Pendleton

January 18, 1982

Dear Mr. Pendleton:
    *How thoughtful of you to honor me with the kind of
sage wisdom which, to be sure, must be that of one who has
never, in his entire life, made a mistake.*
    *Only one so flawless could presume, from the scant
newspaper items he has read, that I need to "get well"; that
all those arrested on D.W.I. charges <u>have</u> to be alcoholics,
and that such people cannot possibly be penitent, remorse-
ful, humiliated and shamed by such an unthinking act.*
    *Available to the public, in the files of the Department
of Public Safety, are the names and addresses of all those
citizens who have similarly offended. Perhaps the good-
ness of your spirit will honor them with the same constructive advice you have accorded me.*
                Sincerely,

                Dave Moore

10/13/84

Dear David Moore
    On your Friday (Oct. 12) 6 pm News you made a state-
ment to Fairbourn (in humor supposedly) "that it is this

kind of weather (drizzly & gray) that makes Finns and Icelanders drink so much." We were surprised and disappointed to hear you make the above statement. We differ with you. For one thing, you are wrong about Finlands' weather and secondly the Finns have their drinking crowd like every other country but the general population is not a drinking people.

Sincerely,

W. J. Kortesmaki

W.J. Kortesmaki

October 15, 1984

Dear Mr. Kortesmaki,

Your are right. It was a silly and intemperate remark for me to have made, and the moment it got out of my mouth I wanted to call it back.

It was a particularly absurd indiscretion since I offered no facts or source to support it.

My personal "source" is a friend who has done business extensively in both Finland and Iceland for years. He claims that the incidence of alcoholism in those countries is inordinately high, and that the long periods of dreary weather is a factor.

Fact or not, I recognize that the stupidity of the comment was compounded by the cavalier, off-handed manner in which it was delivered.

I appreciate your taking the time to point it out, and I should appreciate your showing this letter to friends who may have been similarly offended.

Sincerely,

Dave Moore

The following exchange refers to an Edina motorist who, after driving her car into an inconspicuously located chain link fence, notified authorities of potential danger — and was made to pay for the damage.

2/1/83

Dave Moore:
Your final item on the 10 P.M. news last night about the chain link fence damage reflected more emotionalism than intelligent thought.
Which taxpayers do you propose pay for the damage? Or do you suggest that the damage not be repaired? If I understood the item correctly, Edina did not render the bill.
Lastly, your "Idiots!" at the end was extremely unprofessional.

Gene Felton

P.S. I live in Edina, too.

February 2, 1983

Dear Mr. Felton,
Now, in the clear light of my subsided rage from Monday night, I must agree with you that my deportment was quite "unprofessional."
It wasn't my original intent to use the word "idiots" at the end of the piece, but I found, as I read along, I became increasingly outraged, and being human, and being a citizen of Edina, I could not help myself.
To answer your question: certainly the residents of Edina should pay for the repair. Or the county, or the state, or whomever. But surely not the person who had the accident! Here she was kind enough to warn of the treacherous

71

area, honest enough to give her name and address and then fined ninety dollars for her thoughtfulness.

Correct: Edina did not "render the bill" but gave the information to the State, which did! Now I'm getting angry all over again.

Sincerely,

Dave Moore

August 4, 1983

Dear Dave:-

My family and I have been fans of your for many years — ever since you started at WCCO, in fact. We have been strong boosters of you too.

A reporter has the duty to report the news in a fair and unbiased manner. I thought you had pretty much done this — at least, compared with many other so-called reporters — Although in the last couple years have noticed a tendency on your part to occasionally steer news in favor of the liberal, left-wing political positions.

The other evening you reported the item of Congressman Frenzel being appointed chairman of a committee to curb misuse of the congressional franking privileges, and then observed that you had learned this from a newsletter released by Frenzel at government expense. A very sarcastic and damaging report, wasn't it. But you deliberately avoided reporting that *all* members have and use this franking privilege but that some of them are grossly and excessively using it for their own advantage, and most of them are the liberal big-spending members.

Your bias against the conservative (Republican) party was clearly portrayed. When I heard it, I reached forward and flipped the TV set to another station.

It is sad to see a reporter of your ability succumb to your personal bias in your work and thereby disqualifying yourself as a reporter. The people deserve unbiased reporting and I think you would be surprised at the amount of people who are sick of the media's relentless shaping the news to fit the liberal cause.

I'll grant you it is exceedingly difficult to find unbiased news reporting today since ninety-percent of the news media are liberal. And I do not quarrel with your right to have your political preference. But you do have the professional duty to *report news in an unbiased way.* You now fail in this duty and are reduced to the same level as many other run-of-the-mill reporters.

Goodbye Dave. "Turning off" is forever.

Yours truly,

Finn T. Heimdahl

August 9, 1983

Dear Mr. Heimdahl:

I am sorry your sensibilities were offended by the manner in which we reported Congressman Frenzel's appointment to the House Franking Committee.

Since a major responsibility of the committee is to police congressional abuses of the free postage policy, and since its chairman dispatched his message postage-free, the intent was to read the item with some sense of irony. There was no "sarcasm" nor was any intended.

But your complaint is well taken and it was poor judgement on my part to deal with the item in such an offhanded and frivolous manner.

However are you not guilty of the same charge you have levelled at me? Are you not similarly reckless when you insist that "ninety-percent of the news media are liberal?" How come you by such a figure? Are you privy to information that would substantiate such a childish and ludicrous charge?

I am sure you'll be satisfied with whatever local channel you choose for your news and information. We in the Twin Cities are fortunate to have several excellent options.

Dave Moore

August 11, 1983

Dear Sir:-

Your letter of the 9th. Thanks for taking the time to reply to my recent criticism.

A comment about my "childish and ludicrous charge that ninety-percent of the news media are liberal." For your info, at least two or three studies or surveys have been made in recent years, revealing that eighty-five-percent to ninety-percent (one was even higher if not mistaken) of the news reporters and writers are liberal ... Right at your own station isn't it a pretty safe bet that most, if not all, are liberal ... So your shock at my statement kind of smells a little bit to me.

At least I have you pegged right don't I? Left, that is.

Yours truly,

Finn T. Heimdahl

P.S. Have been too harsh in my judgement of you, I guess, and no doubt it stems from my complete frustration with the news media in general. Just want you to know that it has come across the screen clearly these many years that you are a very decent human being and turning to another station has not been done without a nagging sense of loss.

December 13, 1983

Dear Dave,

I admire the leadership role that WCCO TV has taken in the Twin Cities by attempting to present comprehensive news programs, and I have observed with great pleasure WCCO's obvious affirmative action program. I commend WCCO TV for this fine accomplishment.

While watching the 10 PM news program on December 7, 1983, I was particularly dismayed to hear your derogatory remark about Government Employees. Poking fun at Government Employees at all levels has become too easy over the years. As a Federal Employee I find that my fellow workers are intelligent, hard-working, highly moral individuals who are quick to admit mistakes. I have worked in private enterprise and my experience shows me that Government workers are as good as they come.

Quite frankly, I have strayed a considered distance from Commercial News sources to Public Radio's "All Things Considered" because I don't hear the type of snyde comments you made.

My hope is that your considerable professionalism will carry you above this unnecessary type of editorialism in the future. It doesn't wear well on you.

Sincerely,

John F. Blackstone, P.E.

December 21, 1983

Dear Mr. Blackstone:

I am truly sorry our little tease about bureaucrats offended you. But since you work in government I can certainly understand your dismay.

However, I am sure you're aware that since the beginning of time, government — any government — with its entangling bureaucracies has been the source of satire, parody and joke.

The early Greek playwrights, Aeschylus, Euripides, Aristophanes, teased bureaucrats. Shakespeare, Tolstoy, Mark Twain, all took their shots at government. Will Rogers made a living twitting bureaucrats. Bob Hope still does.

As a newscaster, I know what it is to be teased. Who takes more good natured abuse than the weatherman? Certainly no one really disparages your work, Mr. Blackstone, least of all those of us who must deal with government.

For what it's worth, I, too, am a fan of All Things Considered — have been for years. In my view it is the only genuine news and public information program in the broadcast media.

Sincerely,

Dave Moore

The following is a commentary broadcast on the occasion of the major league All Star game about to be played at the Metrodome, wherein one key word, used just twice, brought but one letter. I had hope for more.

All Star Commentary

(LIVE ON DAVE)	Thank God for the All Star game — I think only She can save baseball from itself.
(TAKE SILENT VTR — WILLIE MAYS HOMERS)	Since the 1965 event in Bloomington where we watched Willie Mays smash Camilo Pascual's second pitch of the game 450 feet into the stands...
(LIVE ON DAVE)	... the All Star game has pretty much remained intact — even though its primary participants are selected by mindless fans witlessly punching holes in cards for their favorite, undeserving players in ballots handed out at the ball parks. It's a paradox: baseball's tossing out the reserve clause, which released the players from bondage, put team ownership into the hands of the tycoon, because he had the financial
(LIVE ON DAVE)	... wherewithal (as well as the bad judgement) to pay outlandish wages to claw-handed infielders who will never hit higher than their bowling averages.
(TAKE SILENT VTR — CALVIN G.)	Minnesota can lay claim to the last of the base ball oriented owners, who held steadfast against the all-consuming tentacles of what we call progress.
(LIVE ON DAVE)	I ask God to protect me from further "progress" ... such as designated hit-

76

ters and fields with roofs on them. I
ask Her to save me from the fate of
living long enough to hear a small boy
say to his father, "Jimmy's dad saw a
baseball game that *he* said was
played *outdoors*! Do you believe
that??"

(TAKE VTR: METRO-
DOME LONG SHOT
ZOOM IN ON IT)

July 31, 1985

Dear Dave:

I wish with this note to express my appreciation for
your truly remarkable career as a Channel 4 anchorman.
At the same time, I wish to call your attention to an article,
"God's Common Name" in the August issue of the ALC's
Lutheran Standard magazine.

On page four of the article, the author writes: "Calling
God "she" or "her" is jarring — it doesn't seem to work."

Remembering your pre-All Star Game channel 4 commentary (in which you twice referred to God as "she"), I
merely wished to let you know that for this listener the
feminizing of God was indeed *jarring—it didn't seem
to work*.

Now, I realize the debate over which pronoun to use
with God has just begun, and it should be very interesting
to watch as the discussion unfolds. In my opinion, James
Nestingen, author of "God's Common Name," provides
some helpful insights.

Thanks for listening, and best wishes in the days
ahead.

Sincerely,

John R. Nyberg

John R. Nyberg

August 2, 1985

Dear Mr. Nyberg,

Thank you for your thoughtful note, and particularly for enclosing Mr. Nestingen's article. If one is committed to total acceptance of the Bible, he certainly offers strong arguments for thinking of God in the masculine gender.

However since I fancy myself as neither Christian, Jew, Moslem, Hindu or Brahmin — I respect all of those outfits and I think each of them has good points going for them — I feel free to keep my options open.

Calling God "She" may be jarring to Mr. Nestingen but not to me. I rather like it.

In all candor, I used the "She" pronoun to see if anyone would react. I am disappointed that you have been the only one. On the other hand, perhaps we should feel a positive message from that: that when one deals with God, gender is a trivial consideration.

I certainly do appreciate your taking the time to write.

Dave Moore

August 24, 1977

Dear Dave,

I wish you would quit talking negatively about the Twins. Because the Twins are drawing good crowds I'm sure many fans are disgusted with your criticism. Monday night you complained about the Twins losing ground-when in fact they won and therefore did not lose ground. The other day you complained because they fell to fourth place. Would you rather see them in second place ten games out of first? The night they scored eleven runs in one inning you complained because they won the game by a close margin — a win is good no matter what the score. Another night you cut them down because they lost to lowly Seattle. Do you expect us to win them all? I remind you the team that wins the World Series this year will probably have lost seventy games before they're crowned World Champions and will have lost some games to the poor teams. You have no knowledge of baseball as evidenced by your statements.

The Twins would be much better off if the media gave them full support.

Sincerely yours,

Gary A. Beckmann

Gary A. Beckmann

August 26, 1977

Dear Mr. Beckmann,

While I can understand and appreciate your feelings regarding my remarks about the Twins, I cannot sympathize with them.

As I indicated on the air last night — and I certainly don't take you to task for your letter — I take the position of the fan, which I have been for forty-five years.

Since I am not a sportscaster, or one who makes a living in that field, I believe I am entitled to that prerogative. Certainly I wouldn't act in such a way were I the sportscaster, for then I could be compromising the objectivity of my position.

But I don't <u>have</u> to be objective. Don't you see? I am the Fan. It's an American tradition that Baseball and the Weather are subjects on which each of us is allowed to vent our feelings.

And I don't think the Twins are going to be inspired to win or lose by my railings, which are, at worst, and do, more often than not, reflect the kind of unreasonableness born of frustration. Frustration does not always produce sensible statements.

Sincerely,

Dave Moore

June 10, 1986

Dear Dave:

I have sometimes noticed that during your lead-ins to stories about my lawsuit against the legislature, your statements are not entirely accurate.

In fact, I have said since March, 1983, in a public letter to all two-hundred-and-one members of the legislature and the six constitutional officers, that my office should be combined with the offices of State Auditor and Secretary of State. I have said repeatedly since March, 1983, that such a merger should be accomplished only by way of a constitutional amendment *approved by the voters*, which is required by the Minnesota consitution. I have never advocated that the legislature abolish my office or any other constitutionally elected office.

I have also said repeatedly that certain of the duties of the treasurer, until recently repealed by the legislature, should remain with an elected official.

I can understand that all of this is somewhat arcane and how you and your writers might become a bit confused. This letter is just for your own information, so you know the facts as this story continues to develop.

Sincerely,

Robert W. Mattson

June 11, 1986

Dear Mr. Mattson,

A fascinating facet of this work is that no matter how long one works at it, one learns something every day.

Except me, it seems.

Your letter embarrasses me. In reading the script before air time I should have caught the mistake. It should have been familiar to me since I MADE PRECISELY THE SAME ERROR ONCE BEFORE!! When it first became an issue.

The first time I plead ignorance of the matter. In this case it was strictly a loss of concentration.

I am thankful, at least, that Marcia (Fleur) made the issue clear in the body of her report: that your proposal calls for an amendment to be put before the voters.

The calmed civility of your letter is a noble exercise in restraint and I appreciate your forebearance in the matter.

Dave Moore

October 20, 1983

Dear Dave:

I must take you to task for your pronunciation of Chandrasekhar's name when you reported his winning the Nobel Prize. Anyone who has contributed as much as Chandra, and who has won the Prize, deserves to have his name pronounced correctly.

When there is a question like this one, you or a member of your staff could call the Department of Astronomy and set it straight.

Sincerely yours.

Edward P. Ney
Regents' Professor of Physics
and Astronomy
University of Minnesota

October 24, 1983

Dear Dr. Ney

I am grateful to you for calling my attention to the Chandrasekhar mispronunciation. but it would have been more helpful to me had you provided me with the proper pronunciation.

It is not a name that comes up in our day-to-day conversation.

United Press International and Associated Press were at odds on the matter: AP favored accent on the middle syl-

lable (DRA). UPI went with the last syllable (KAHR).

*To tell you the truth I don't recall how I pronounced it
— I think I was just happy to get through it. Perhaps
you'll enlighten me.*

Sincerely,

Dave Moore

January 6, 1984

Dear Mr. Moore:

I watched your newscasts on January 4 and 5, which
included segments on the proposed domestic partnership
legislation in Minneapolis and the public outcry against
Dan White, the convicted killer of San Francisco's mayor
and gay city supervisor.

I was surprised by your repeated use of the word homosexual in those stories. That word, I think, is best used in
a story on sexual behavior; the very word sex is in the middle of homosexual. But what does sex have to do with polit-
ically determined access to insurance benefits or mass
community response to a political murder?

I think in both cases a less sexual word would have
been more appropriate. I suggest the word gay, since many
gay people prefer that word, just as many black people prefer black over Negro.

You may wonder why I make the distinction. Continued use of the word homosexual to describe gay people or
gay activities reduces gays to nothing more than sexual
animals. Don't you think that heterosexuals would dislike
being defined solely on the basis of their private sexual behavior? The same holds true for gays. Gay relationships
can be sexual, of course, but they can also be built on love,
intimacy, romance, compatability, a sense of family,
commitment.

I would respect your newscasts more if you presented a
more accurate portrait of gays as total people whose news-
worthiness is often based not on their sexual behavior, but
on the impact of their asexual activity in politics, culture,

religion, business and social services. Why must the thinking people who watch Channel 4 be subjected to sexual catchwords that only detract from accurate news coverage?

Thank you for your consideration of this matter.

Sincerely,

Eric W. Stults

Eric W. Stults

January 11, 1984

Dear Mr. Stults:

Regarding your letter of January 6th: until recent years the word "gay" has been accessible to all of us. I have become increasingly incensed that a particular segment of society has not only comandeered the word to define its own sexual preference, but in so doing, has rendered it obsolete for the rest of us.

Today the word, "gay" evokes snickers when used in its original, appropriate context, that is, to describe a state of emotion.

I disagree with your contention that the word "sex" is "best used in a story on sexual behavior." On the contrary, "sex" is a word with niether pejorative nor negative connotations. The word distinguishes gender. It appears on application blanks to identify male and female. "Homosexual" is a word that faultlessly and accurately defines a kind of gender preference.

Historically, I can find nowhere in the now classic writings of Oscar Wilde, E.M. Forster or Noel Coward — to name but three homosexual authors — a reference to "gay" as a means of describing sexual presuasion and/or preference.

To clarify one other point: in our newscasts homosexuals are not so identified, except in those stories where homosexuality is the crux of the story. Senator Allan Spear, for instance, is not identified as a homosexual when he is engaged in other legislative or academic matters.

I grieve that my stand has cost me the friendship of some very close homosexual friends whose companionship

I have enjoyed for many years. And, alas, that it seems to have cost Channel 4 your viewership. But, so be it.

Dave Moore

Footnote: Had I known at the time that the following letter and response was to be included in a book, I would have pointed out that my obstinate stand would have lost me even more friends, as I'm sure it will.

In the Introduction to this section I stated the citizen vitriol toward the television newscast did not reach "quantitative heights until the late sixties." However the *nature* of displeasure was just as severe in the earlier days.

I wish to conclude this section with a return to a day in June of 1957 — just one month after becoming the ten o'clock newscaster — to my first, genuine, heart-felt letter of wrath. In this case it was not inspired by reasons of "nature of the beast" or (as far as I can determine) the off-handed ad-lib, but rather, it would seem, by my very own, personal air of despicability.

Too thumb-worn to reproduce in its original form, I have re-typed it. I want to be sure we get all the words.

D. Moore
Why can't you shut up. Forty-five minutes we get of your blabbing...how much time do you give the weather guy, Krayling (sic)...or that gentleman Hal Scott or that nice Skip Loescher. Hardly anything at all..it's always Dave Moore yak yak yak. It was bad enough years ago for fifteen minutes. You are a rotten guy and don't deserve....

Here food stain smudgings, dirty thumb prints (probably mine in both cases) and time have made the remainder of the letter indicipherable. The letter was signed by a man whose adddress was simply "Hugo, Minn."

In a sense, I suppose, we owe him our thanks for sparing us the task of reading between the lines.

In response to such letters that defy humane reply, George Rice, WCCO's first designated editorialist — preceding Al Austin and Ron Handberg — devised a form letter:

Dear Mr. So-and-So:

We are obliged to inform you that some idiot is using your name to send scurillous material through the mail. It might be advisable to check with your attornies since there are postal laws protecting the use of the mails against the relay of defamatory messages.

4

Children

What I wouldn't give to have that letter from Halsey Hall!! I'm sure I tucked it in with my baseball cards in the wooden Kraft Cheese box that I kept on the top shelf of my closet. It must have been among many oddments that went into Harry Bright's trash-collecting truck when my parents moved from the family home on West Minnehaha Parkway twenty years later.

It was the summer of 1934. I was ten and sick-a-bed with something or other, listening to Halsey's on-the-spot re-creation of a Minneapolis Millers' road game in Louisville, or Indianapolis. That is, the Millers were playing elsewhere and Halsey was in the WCCO radio studio calling the game, play-by-play, as it unraveled, pitch-by-pitch off a Western Union ticker. A recording of a stadium crowd murmured in the background, its volume rising or fading to accomodate the changing action of play as Halsey described it. Behind Halsey's voice, a make-shift sound effects gadget created the sound of bat meeting ball. In later years, first Dick Enroth and then Ray Christensen would hone and perfect the magic to an even more polished state than Halsey had.

But Halsey was the only practitioner at the time and he was wondrous! He put you right there in that game! Right alongside him. I was not altogether taken in: I knew the Millers were in Louisville and Halsey was downtown in a radio studio, but I didn't know *how* it was done.

From my sick bed I wrote him a letter asking him to clue me in. A very short time later, perhaps no more than a week, came the reply, describing the procedure as I have outlined it to you.

Retrospect makes the memory even more cherished: here was this seasoned, newspaper-scarred veteran — he must have been at least fifty years old! — taking the time to reveal to a ten year old kid the secrets of a mystical broadcasting routine which would remain secret forever to hundreds of thousands of folks a lot older than ten!

Forgive my taking such a circuitous route to explain why letters from children receive my immediate attention.

In sifting the mountainous collection of correspondence for this book, I came across the following, dated, I think, May, 1957.

Dear Mr. Moore,

On your news broadcast when there is any kind of explosion you say you are not sure what causes it, but you say it maybe gas. My dad works for Minnesota Valley Gas. And after customers hear the news they start calling saying they smell gas. My dad goes there and there is no gas smell. So could you please quit saying Maybes unless you are sure.

Tom O.

As I recall I wrote the young man congratulating him on his perceptions, and thanking him for performing a public service, which he indeed had. Since that day I have made it a point to double-check all those news stories of explosions in which it is not more than surmised that gas may have been a factor.

March 11, 1985

Dear Mr. Moore,

Our fourth grade class is involved in quite a project. We are writting letters to fourth graders in each state. We hope to learn about our country and also tell others Minnesota.

Since you have been reporting the news in Minnesota for a number of years, we hope you will help us as we collect information about our state. Would you like to. Any information you give us will be included in our letters as we "spread the word" about Minnesota.

What are the most important news stories you have covered?

What are the greatest challenges facing Minnesota?

What do you like most about Minnesota?

What would you change about our state if you could?

Thank you very much for your time.

Sincerely,

Stacia Herrala

Stacia Herrala

March 15, 1985

Dear Stacia,

Thank you for including me in your survey. What a good idea to contact fourth graders in other states! What better way to discover the differences in our many states. This is the best way to do it at your age. When you are old enough you can travel and find out first hand.

Well — let's see if I can help:

The most important news stories: no one story in particular, but generally many of the business stories to be found In Minnesota. Did you know, for instance — and I think this is something children in other states would find interesting: Minneapolis-St.Paul is the home office (or headquarters) for five of the most successful business firms, or companies in the entire world? General Mills, Pillsbury, 3M, Honeywell and Control Data. There are many others.

Our weather is always an important story — the changing of seasons — getting as hot as one-hundred de-

grees and as cold as thirty below zero! That kind of weather range is probably found in no more than five or six other states.

The greatest challenges facing Minnesota:

I think there are two major challenges: (1) because of our severe winter weather and the high taxes it is difficult to convince businesses — many small businesses, not the kind I have listed on the other page — to locate here. We can't do anything about the weather. But we can adjust our tax system so that many small businesses are not required to may so much in taxes. You'll probably have to ask your teacher more about that — it gets very complicated, this tax business.

The other challenge is to keep our education (or school systems) in high gear. To do this we must offer teachers better pay (it's very upsetting to me that television newscasters and ball players — to name just two jobs — are paid several hundred times more than teachers, whose work is far more important than either of those other two works.)

What do I like most about Minnesota?

Autumn. August through November. There is no other place like it in the world during that time of year.

What would I change about our state, if I could.

Winter. December through March. There is no other place like it in the world during that time of year.

I wish you well in your project. It is a very worthwhile one and I think you must have a pretty wise teacher to suggest it to you.

Dave Moore

Two years ago Paul Adelmann of our news staff produced a three-part series which, in effect, wondered aloud about the possibility of ghosts in some of the older homes of the Twin Cities. Despite the generally whimsical tone to the reports, there were serious overtones. Enough to prompt the following.

Dear, DAVE MOORE
Your Ad, About the ghost series scared me. I don't think you Should have had it on when Kids could watch! Please don't do it again!

BRendan Riley

Thanks from Brendan Riley
Age 7

February 1, 1985

Dear Brendan,

I am truly sorry that our series of reports on Ghosts frightened you.

But you needn't have been: for some reason people seem to feel that Ghosts must be wicked and evil.

They aren't at all. They don't have to be wicked and mean. I'm sure for every kind and loving LIVING person there are as many kind and loving ghosts.

Who says ghosts must frighten people. I have never seen one, but how many people have?

Sincerely,

Dave Moore

In the summer of 1984 our news cameras were on hand when a wrecking ball slammed down the venerable Curtis Hotel on 10th street in downtown Minneapolis.

The camera was situated a considerable distance from the action, a long shot. As we looked at the video tape we saw the crushing of one tall wing of the hotel. As we gazed at the other wing, standing erect, awaiting the wrecking ball — we're speaking of just a matter of seconds — we saw a room window, high up on that second wing, mysteriously go up! As though someone had been in that room, raising the window!

On subsequent newscasts we re-played that portion of the video tape many times, looking for clues.

The incident inspired many bad jokes and this letter.

Dear Mr. Dave Moore,

I would stil Like to Know who Opened Up That window before They blew up the Curtis Hotel? Did some old bum go in their for the night? Thank you,

Anna Tierney

Anna Tierney
Grade 3

July 11, 1984

Dear Anna —

In our questioning of some of the construction engineers who were involved in the implosion of the Curtis Hotel, we were told that the window raising in the second Curtis tower was caused by the pressure from the implosion of the <u>first</u> tower — the tower adjacent to the second tower.

At least no bodies were to be found in the debris below. But it certainly was an eerie happening, wasn't it?

As a native of Minneapolis, I am heart-sick by the blowing-up and tearing down of all these wonderful city structures that were such a loving part of my very happy youth. And so I like to think that the window was raised by a sorrowful but magical hand, to let the workers know that what they are doing — destroying the past — is an <u>evil</u> doing.

I hope you're enjoying your summer.

Dave Moore

5

TV News as Catalyst

Nothing works better than television that works for the good of all. I can think of nothing in my thirty-five years as a television newscaster that has given me more satisfaction — than having my name attached to our documentary series, "The Moore Reports."

To be sure, the designation has built-in complications and embarrassments, since my contribution to the series has been minimal. The voice behind the pictures is mine. The pictures and the message, the total concept and production is the work of many, many brilliant and dedicated men and women who, literally speaking, turn over their lives, for an extended period of time to the job of interpreting, reporting and clarifying the troublesome and puzzling issues of day-to-day community life.

Playing but a small role in such dedication gives me a wonderful advantage: it permits me impunity to agree with those who contend the programs are "network quality."

One such effort was presented in January of this year. "Suffer The Children" documented the disspiriting and frightening uncertainties in the lives of six unwed mothers, five of them lacking the kind of intellectual, social wherewithal that might help them better cope with life as welfare recipients.

As most interpretations of touchy issues do, this one brought on a flood of mail. I have selected the letters of two women whose contrasting but equally troubling circumstances best exemplify how commercial television, used judiciously, can serve as worthwhile catalyst.

Arriving in the same day's mail were letters from Belinda Martinez and Diane Hightower each reacting to the documentary.

Don't be frightened-off by the length of Ms. Martinez' letter. I don't recall a more eloquent or soulful thesis describing both the surface and subliminal side of effects of welfare. I would think it a valuable addition to the professional case worker's portfolio, if not a helpful work-study for the student of social welfare. No less so is the more compacted commentary of Ms. Bradford-Tveraa.

Thursday, January 30, 1986

Dear Mr. Moore,

I wish I could say that I was comforted by the message of the recent special, "Suffer the Children." However, I was not. I found myself becoming more sullen as the show progressed, knowing that I fit into the statistics that were supposedly typified by those women who were chosen to represent the poverty stricken in our area.

I wish that I could see someone chosen who is intelligent enough to speak out on behalf of the suffering children that the story was describing.

I am a divorced mother of one child. I have been on AFDC for eight-and-a-half years. When people hear about the government's statistics designating poverty levels, what they don't know is that AFDC people are living at nearly one-half that figure! Yet the children at these levels suffer from much more than what the lack of money denies them. Sometimes these factors are not clearly represented in such a program.

I had several specific reactions to some parts of the television special. I could not sympathize with the women who were complaining that their food stamps didn't last through the month — when the women who were complaining were overweight. A person doesn't get, or stay fat by not eating. If food was at such a shortage for them, they would certainly have gone more hungry than they look.

I'm not criticizing. There is another side of the coin. Poverty leads to depression. Our lives are so controlled and regulated that it seems as though we have little leeway to improve and little motivation to care. If we lose our motivation to care then we don't tend to ourselves properly. We can eat, drink, smoke, etc. to excess using up our resources and thus feeling worse.

I took offense to being represented by a women who couldn't even keep track of her welfare I.D. in order to cash her check. I believe in the program her words were, "It usually comes to this each month." Well it doesn't have to. Part of the suffering is the stigma that comes from generalizations such as these.

We're called "a broken home" so we get treated like one. Because of statistics certain things are more excusable from us — at least understandable or predictable. That is, malnutrition, crime, and irresponsibility. We're expected by some not to pay our bills on time. It is statistically predictable that either we or our children will steal or use drugs or get into trouble some other way. And, yes it happens, but it shouldn't have to. It is expected that our homes should be dirty and depressing. They shouldn't have to. I have been ridiculed at the bank, treated rudely at the grocery store, and with total disrespect at a pharmacy in the course of my being on welfare. That's where the children suffer too — when dignity and hope are slowly eroded away.

Your T.V. cameras will never catch the disgusted glances we receive as we stand in line to cash our checks or wait in line to pay for our groceries with food stamps. Your microphones will never hear the nasty remarks that fall upon our ears. The public won't see what its like to spend the very first day of the welfare system waiting, hoping, answering questions, filling out forms, waiting some more. Children cry and parents sit with blank faces — eyes vacant because life has come to this. The people will never attend an "absent parent interview" and be asked questions about a parent that no longer sees, cares or knows or wants to know about the children. It can be humiliating and depressing. Your cameras didn't show a baby I saw standing in a cold, freezing rain with no shirt or shoes on his feet while his mother talked on a pay phone. He cried pathetically. Your camera didn't show the two year old boy I know who was taken away from his parent because he was left alone while the parent went to the store. He cried

95

hysterically. Your camera cannot possibly film the inner relief we feel when we have survived one more day, one more week, one more month, and for some of us — one more year.

There are extenuating circumstances to poverty that your public will also never know. The husband with a good paying job who left his family of four children and his wife to make it on their own. The battered, beaten wife who has been so injured she seeks shelter and refuge for herself and her child. Abuse takes a long time to undo, but thrown into a poverty situation we never quite get around to it. Some of us have hopes and dreams like regular people, but they fade when we need to live and plan from day to day.

There are real small ways of suffering too. Did you ask any of the women if they could show you photographs of their children? Film and cameras and developing are not in the budget. Did you ask the women how often they send a letter in the mail that didn't have to do with a welfare form or a bill? Stamps cost money too. Did you ask the children how they feel on father's day? My daughter cries — and at school when they work on projects she is very sad. Did you ask the children how they feel when they see their friends do some activity with their father (or mother) and know that they will never even see their's? My daughter grows quiet with that emptiness. Have you ever even wondered how we can teach our children that the way we, of necessity, live is not the way it was meant to be? How can they value a normal, two parent family, when they have never experienced it for themselves? There is more suffering then just what money does not provide.

Last year I had a broken wrist. After the temporary cast was taken off in an orthopedic surgeon's office it was determined that I did need a permanent cast put on. Because I was on medical assistance, I could not have it done right there. I had to go to the emergency room where the same doctor put it on. It's the system. I'll probably be "systemed" to death. But I hope my daughter isn't.

I'm not sure what the answer is, but a good place to start is our self-esteem. Money can't buy that.

I manage. After eight-and-a-half years of this I have learned many ways to get by. It isn't easy and sometimes depression even hits the toughest survivors. The toughest survivors don't cry when they're alone because it goes unheard, and they don't cry with their friends because their friends are in the same boat.

Did you ask the people in the TV special how many friends they have who are not on welfare? We're not generally associated with. And single moms seldom have married women friends of any consistency. How bad could our influence be?

Lastly, Mr. Moore, I'd love to invite you to my home for a chat. You are welcome to come at your convenience. Call me if you would care to do this. Thanks for your time.

Most sincerely,

Belinda Martinez

Belinda Martinez

February 7, 1986

Dear Ms. Martinez,

Four times each year following the broadcast of one of our documentaries, I clear my desk and prepare to dive in to the ton of mail that has poured in in response to the program.

Some of the letters, praising the program, require only a polite "thank you." Others, asking for information, I pass on to our producers. To others, offering severe criticism of the program, I generally, more often than not, I fear, reply defensively.

I don't know how to handle your letter.

I must say that I am somewhat taken aback that someone who writes as eloquently as you is not doing it for a living. I don't recall the last time I received a letter offering such perception and insight to a problem. Perhaps it has something to do with your being a victim of the problem.

And how is it that with your kind of intelligence you have remained a victim for eight-and-a-half years?

Are you able to work? That is, can you work? Are you handicapped, one way or another?

Of all the unmarried mothers who have written to me on the subject you are the only one to mention "self-es-

teem." Is that what has carried you all these years? Is that what has allowed you to stand up against all the stigma you have listed?

While I await some answers I call on you to see what you can do to pass on some of your self-esteem to the woman whose letter I have taken the extreme liberty to enclose.

I have never done such a thing — to invade another's privacy in a very personal matter — but I am convinced that the best help she could receive would be the kind that you could offer. Which is to say nothing of how such a project might help _you_. If only, spiritually.

I have written her, chewing her out, sort of; pointing out to her that what she has done for herself and her family should be a source of pride; the senselessness of ascrbing the pitiable circumstances of others to herself, etc.

Who knows? She may be offended by your writing her. But I think not.

I have preferred not to call you. I tend to be longer-winded on the phone than at the typewriter.

Dave Moore

NOTE: I enclosed the following letter from Diane Hightower.

Fri 31st Jan.

Dear Dave,

This letter concerns the documentary "Suffer The Children" last Monday night.

First let me tell you I'm not blaming you for the anguish it has caused my family. I realize many people are involved in putting a documentary together and you were the narrator.

For many years, thirteen to be exact, I've struggled alone to raise two daughters. The program brought to a head the feelings of hopelessness associated with poverty. On Tuesday my sixteen-year-old took an overdose of pills. The program gave the impression there is not even a flicker of light at the end of the tunnel. When hope is taken away people have nothing. This documentary was devastating to us.

My daughter has seen me struggling to finish college, which I did last quarter. Now I'm out I find I'm too poor to buy clothes or gas to look for work and I've thousands in loans to repay. This program was viewed at a crucial turning point in our lives.

We feel the middle class were educated at the expense of a group of poor women. I don't feel this documentary helped people to understand & it deserves a follow up on issues concerning the lack of resources for poor people.

My children have a real social conscience. They write to congressmen, volunteer at a place for the homeless, and donate time to the YWCA. Even the thirteen-year-old daughter who is a high potential child was crying and asking me "does this mean there's no hope, thats what they said. how am I going to college?" Our worse fears were realized on Monday night.

Dave, I've been a loyal fan of yours for years & cried with you at the ceremony honoring you. Please write us a letter. I know that documentary did not start out to have the consquences it had on my family & probably many others in similar situations. If the producers had known I doubt they would have bothered to make it.

Thank you for reading my letter. I'm still a loyal fan of yours.

Sincerely,

Diane Hightower

Diane Hightower

February 4, 1986

Dear Ms. Hightower,
    I am sorry our program proved so upsetting to you, although I must say, despite your history, I don't know why it should have been.
    I don't understand how you can be devastated by circumstances that not only are not yours, but not even similar to yours.

In fact, I would think that you and your daughters would have gained some solace from the program. That foremost in their minds would be the thought, "There, but for the strength and determination of our Mom, go we! "But she wouldn't let that happen!"

You have set them a wonderful example, and I would think that with your encouragement they would act on it. Can't they (and you) see what you have done? Despite the mos't adverse of conditions you have put yourself through school and kept your fine family together. The women portrayed in our documentary have no glimmer of hope.

I'm sorry I cannot write you further. There are simply too many others — without your strength and will — whose letters require responses.

Dave Moore

February 13, 1986

Dear Mr. Moore,

Thank-you for your response to my letter. I can tell by your questions that you have taken an interest in my personal circumstances. In my evaluation of your documentary, I deliberately chose to leave out such subjective details because reciting a litany of my personal hardships would not have served you in any way whatsoever. A "poor me" attitude narrows the range of focus — no matter what the subject of discussion. What we need to solve problems is a wide perspective of things before we zero in on a target area for improvement. It was with that overall objectivity that I tried to evaluate your documentary.

I can, at this time, however, answer the questions you have directed towards me. I have remained a victim, as you say, for several reasons. I was thrust into poverty literally overnight. As a young wife, about three weeks pregnant, I was beaten up by my husband. While I was in the hospital trying not to miscarry, he withdrew all our money from the bank and left. I was discharged from the hospital to a battered women's shelter. During my three week stay I set some long-range goals that I *never* lost sight of despite the turmoil that was to follow. The most important goal was to raise my child to have a sense of family even though all the statistics would be against us. The welfare system supports this by at least allowing the single parent to remain at home until the child's sixth birthday. I decided that since she would likely *never* know her father she would need some strong family roots from me and I chose to *not* put her in daycare or pre-school so we could really get to know each other. I have also very rarely left her with a babysitter. *I* wanted to be the one to see her first steps. *I* wanted to be the one to teach her to talk. *I* wanted to be the one to teach her right from wrong. It was time well-spent, Mr. Moore! I am quite proud of her.

That single goal accounts for the first six-and-a-half years of my poverty. The last two years have been quite another story entirely. It seems that the abuse I suffered was more extensive than I even knew at the time. In the past two years I have had surgeries to correct the damage incurred. I had broken bones in my neck, torn discs, and a badly damaged nerve that left one arm immobile for months. My most recent surgery was in June at which time I was in the hospital thirty days. That was the third time the neurosurgeon had gone into my neck. I have been in physical therapy almost daily since then. Those physical problems account for the last part of my poverty. Was I able to work? Mr. Moore, I could not even dress myself or comb my hair. My six-year-old helped me! By the grace of God that total incapacity was relatively short lived. I have come a long way. The pain has been excruciating for months on end — yet all the while I was still a single mom with the same household to run. We have managed. I had to remind myself daily that my worth was not measured by the fact that I couldn't scrub my floor or wash all my dishes at one time. My worth was not measured by the fact that I needed as many as four naps each day and twelve hours of sleep each night. These are hard lessons to learn no matter what economic level we're in. Self-esteem is an important commodity.

I have an infectious laugh and a hardy sense of humor that has not ebbed away as the time of poverty adds day onto day. I have compassion without any limitations to it. My nickname used to be "energy woman" because I attacked life zealously. That zest is still there, but it has, of necessity, been turned inward temporarily, until my body recovers from the war waged against it.

You asked me if I am handicapped. I have been. Right now it is more like a disabilty, the permanance of which is not known. I am working very hard at getting well. *I would love nothing better than to work!* I am not a lazy person — employment will be a welcome change to my lifestyle! But in defense of myself I must say — even being on welfare, I have always been busy (when physically able.) I put in a few hours at a hospital each week, I help at church, I look for one small way each day that I can be of assistance to someone who is on this earth with me. I believe all of this will be to my benefit. When it comes to filling out a resumé, it will be at such a time that I hope my Heavenly Employer will be able to inspire a good recommendation!

It would seem that my gift of articulation and insight offer me more authority than I can sometimes take responsibility for. Your request of me (to write to Diane Hightower) was a threatening challenge — for about an hour! Then I dove in. I took her letter, line-by-line and tried to give her some constructive feedback. For better, or worse, I have done as you asked. I really do thank you for asking me to be of assistance.

I *sincerely* wish we could have lunch together sometime, Mr. Moore . . . I could sit and talk with you as easily as I could with Archbishop Roach, or a psychologist, or a businessman from 3M or a person standing in line for food at the Dorothy Day Center. Poverty doesn't have to make us shallow people . . .

Feel free to call upon me again if I can be of assistance. I look forward to hearing from you again. Until such time, I remain

Sincerely yours,

Belinda Martinez

Belinda Martinez

February 18, 1986

Dear Ms. Martinez,

First of all, thank you for acting on my request to Ms. Hightower. As you, I wait her response, if any. I think it may have been a bit to write initially to me, so I'm sure the response to you will not be immediately forthcoming.

I don't see have she can help but get some solace from it. Indeed, it is so well written that it could serve as a spiritual guide to other women in similar circumstances.

I regret, that for the nonce I must decline your invitation to meet with you. The way my schedule is running now it's all I can do to stay ahead: aside from a class at the University, occasional freelance work, the demands of myriad charity requests — to say nothing of a regular work schedule here, have forced me to confine my social time to my family.

But I hope we can stay in touch and again I thank you for the time _you_ have taken from _your_ heavy schedule.

Dave Moore

Monday, February 24, 1986

Dear Mr. Moore,

Thank you for your recent letter. I am pleased to know that you approved of my letter to Ms. Hightower. I took the bull by the horns this very evening and extended myself further by calling her home. She was not in, however I spoke to her sixteen-year-old daughter, Karen, to whom she had referred in her letter to you. Karen knew who I was because her mother shared my letter with both daughters. We chatted for a while about how she's doing and I believe she will be fine. She took my phone number and had her mother return my call. We have just completed our conversation after an hour talk. I am glad I made the call and I just wanted you to know that I had involved myself slightly more than you asked.

It would seem that my recent communication with you is turning out to be quite timely in light of what's going on in the State House of Representatives. One thing that you and I have mentioned is self-esteem, the maintanance of which can be virtue. St. Thomas Aquinas said a long time ago that a decent sufficiency of this world's goods is necessary for the practice of virtue. A thirty-percent AFDC cut would certainly deplete what I would consider a decent supply of this world's goods. I would be homeless. Giving me more food stamps is not the answer — I don't need more food stamps if I'm not going to have a place to eat!

I wish that I could speak — not in angry opposition — but in humble and firm disapproval. The right people are being presented with the right statistics but the despair cannot be tallied. It is that despair that must speak. I find little consolation in knowing that lady Liberty still stands as a visible symbol for national compassion. The poem by Emma Lazarus engraved at the base of the statue reads in part; "Give me your *tired*, your *poor*, Your huddled masses yearning to breathe free; the wretched refuse of your teaming shore"...etc. Well, Mr. Moore — *we're already here! I am* tired. I haven't given up hope, but I'm tired of having to hold on so tightly. I *am* poor. On Thursday at 12 noon in the capitol rotunda you will see the huddled *masses* yearning to breathe free. We are not free except free to sleep in the street or free to starve. If we were to agree that poverty is the lack of material necessities, then such a drastic cut in AFDC would force me to succumb to poverty. That would increase the powerlessness and immobility that I already know only too well as a result of my economic level. That certainly taints the liberty that we here in America so highly esteem. According to Webster's dictionary inalienable means incapable of being alienated, surrendered or transferred. It would seem that by lowering my (and our) income to such an extent is an attempt to uproot my basic rights from their very core. If we still hold such basic rights as life and liberty so precious, then I must oppose this cut in AFDC because it is destructive of these ends and is not likely to *effect* my Safety and Happiness. Feel free to use this letter if it should become appropriate, so long as it upholds my dignity and does not alter my intent.

I am not at all put off by our unlikelihood of having lunch. I admire people who hold families and responsibilities in high priority! I too would like to remain in touch. I suspect that you will soon be hearing from Ms. Hightower. She was quite appreciative of a second letter she received from WCCO from Robert Thurber. If you have the occasion to call on my assistance again in any way, please let me know. I am quite willing to extend myself when possible.

Sincerely yours,

Belinda Martinez

Belinda Martinez

Feb. 25, 86

Dear Dave,

Since writing to you a number of events have occurred in our lives. Belinda Martinez wrote us a long, encouraging letter and last night I talked to her on the phone. She went to college in Mankato and we have some mutual acquaintances. Someday we hope to meet each other.

Robert Thurber from WCCO wrote us. Knowing people care enough to write thoughtful letters means a great deal to my family.

My daughter Karen is feeling less depressed. The last month and a half have been very trying for many people here. We have been dealing with the suicides of three young people, two from my daughters school. We received Belinda's letter the same day we learned of the suicide of a 15 year old girl who took classes with my daughter. The letter was comforting and your passing our letter on to Belinda may have been unusual but it did work out for the best. I strongly believe people have to get together and draw strength from each other. If the proposed AFDC cuts go through people will need all the help they can get.

My strength and hope have returned and I believe somehow things will work out for my family. Thanks for caring Dave.

Sincerely,

Diane Hightower

Diane Hightower

What would appear to be fitting culmination to this series of correspondence (not to the relationship, one would hope) came to Ms. Martinez from Ms. Hightower on September 1st of this year. Ms. Martinez sent it on to me. I am assuming permission of both women to print it here.

Belinda your letter came at such an important time. Since last winter I have stressed to my daughters how important it is to be suppportive of each other. Some times an act of kindness can come at such a crucial time it is never forgotten.

This past weekend I attended a conference for RUFJ at New Ulm. I don't know if you're familiar with the group. It means Recipients United For Justice. They have hired a state wide organizer and his office is at 17th and Nicollet in Minneapolis. I hope the group grows and gets active here.

Some day I hope we can meet each other. I feel there's a bond with us and I wish you all the best.

Diane Hightower

Diane Hightower

February 4, 1986

Dear Mr. Moore,

As a victim of the castigations of the welfare system, I feel compelled to respond to your show, "Suffer the Children." May the goddess Artemis take her place at your side and continue to shoot her arrows freely in righteous anger.

I am, at this time, a single mother of three enrolled at Minneapolis Community College. Because I have taken the initiative to become educated, my welfare grant and medical benefits are about to be denied. Suffer the children. Because the system we live within will benefit by keeping women in poverty and people of color culturally and intellectually impotent, suffer the children. Because this great country of ours places no value on education, suffer the children.

You have my sincere appreciation for using your influences to try and better educate the people who may, unknowingly, be contributing to the immoral politics of this country.

Sincerely,

[signature: Joan Bradford-Tveraa]

Joan Bradford-Tveraa

February 7, 1986

Dear Ms. Bradford-Tveras,

I would welcome the presence of Artemis by my side — but only if the arrows of her "righteous anger" come closer to the mark than ours have.

If letters from the public are a measurement it can be said that while our audience may have been vast, it was the wrong audience.

Hundreds of letters from unmarried mothers. We don't need to hear from them! Not one letter —at least not to me — from a legislator, a social service director, or public official.

Not one.

Your eloquence on the matter is stunning. You'll do well, I know. Somehow you'll make it. Self esteem can do that.

But what about the others?

[signature: Dave Moore]

Dave Moore

In whatever catalystic way I may have managed, over the years, to impart to correspondents ideas on how to fight the adversity that government imposes on us, there have been others — many others, I fear — whose difficulties have been so overwhelming that I have been rendered by their letters as helpless as they.

One such letter follows. My pithy, cold, and indifferent responses to the woman's very real and maddening plight left me (and has again, upon this re-reading) reeling with self-contempt for refusing to even acknowledge her problems. I can only guess that her circumstances left me baffled: to think that anyone of such civility, such profound intellect and fortitude could be so brutally entrapped by a social system which we like to think is the most just in the world!

January 27, 1986

Dear Mr. Moore,

I watched with interest and frustration you report "Suffer The Children" Monday evening.

My mind is racing. I don't know where to start with everything I want to tell you. It may be a book when I'm through but I still would like to give you my side of the story.

You'll excuse this being handwritten. I cannot afford a typewriter and yet it would be very well used if I could afford one.

To give you a little background. I come from an upper middle class family in another state. I was not physically abused and do not have alcoholic parents.

I'm living in an apartment that when I moved to Minneapolis and this neighborhood I thought was in a good neighborhood and had a good landlord. How wrong I was! A reputable source has told me my landlord is considered *"The Slum Landlord"* of Minneapolis. My apartment is very close to where the lady in the report lives that had the crime meeting with her landlord. As I don't have a car I walk past that building often. My landlord is comparable to most of the landlord's described. Alot like the one that went to court. All they (those types of landlords) care about is money. They do not care about the tenants. If however they do, do something they definitely expect something in return. They also are *very* good at only hearing what they want to hear.

Although I have thermo draperies there is thick ice on the inside of my living room windows tonight. The floor is too cold to walk on. I've been sleeping in flannel pajamas, a warm robe and with *two* quilts, one of which is wool-lined. Tell you anything about the heat we don't get? Yes I realize there are homeless people and that upsets me to a point. That's another issue, but don't you think that if the rent is paid things in the buildings should be taken care of?

Now I'm living on a very fixed income. I get two unemployment checks a month. Out of which I pay rent and have $20.00 a month to live on. Right now I'm getting GA medical and $45.00 a month in food stamps. I don't want to live this way but if you'll read on I'll explain why I am. It also may help to tell you I'm single, never been married, never had children. Now because I'm getting $88.00 a week UC that's too much to get help from GA with the rent. Not that anyone else cares but I have had my cat for 11 years. Food stamps don't cover cat food and litter. Neither do they cover bus fare to look for jobs or transportation to bring groceries home. Nothing they provide covers any paper products or cleaning products. Did you consider putting that in your report? Do you have any idea how embarrassing it is to go to the food shelves? Believe me $45.00 in food stamps doesn't do it either. After going to the same grocery store for two years its also very embarrassing to go there with food stamps.

The first year of my life I couldn't afford Christmas presents for anyone or even a Christmas tree.

Where is this all leading you ask?? I'll tell you. Because I definitely want to better my life and because I want to work and to have a job for longer than three months at a time I started looking for a way to do this. I found CHART and from there METP. Let me say here that when I work which is most of the time I do pay taxes. Anyway I now have a chance to go to school for six months for free to do something I want very much. I've taken all the tests and made the necessary arrangements with the school. Here's where the system really screws you over. Schools set, right? But if I go my unemployment will stop because I won't be available forty hours a week, I probably won't get help from GA and even if I did it won't cover the rent. Right

109

now I would gladly take any help I can get from the agencies just to be able to go to school to get ahead. What I'm going to have to do is get a part time job but let's be honest where am I going to find a job that will cover the rent plus whatever else it will need to cover? Between a rock and a hard place, you bet! If I don't get this chance I'll be right back where I started from and I don't want the rest of my life to be like this part has been. Move to a cheaper apartment you say? To get out of these areas of town I'd pay what I'm paying now if not more. After your report I literally checked the locks on my windows. Not that they're great but they help. Also do you have any idea just how expensive it is to move??

I guess I'm winding down now. I love little children very much and I understand in part why you chose the subjects you did for your story. But what about those of us that were maintaining a better life style and now cannot? What about those of us that want to get ahead, even have that chance but because of the system may not be able to? What about those of us that want to get their landlords to be responsible for their property but are afraid of what will happen if we rock the boat? What about those of us that think the system could be improved upon? What if, what if, what if???

I just wanted to write this to give you a little food for thought from another angle.

Also the way people say the word "welfare" on reports like yours makes those of us on the system that care feel *quite uncomfortable.*

Sincerely,

Kay E. Green

Kay E. Green

February 6, 1986

Dear Ms. Green,

The producers of our documentary, "Suffer The Children" recognize and are certainly not insensitive to all of the "what ifs" you have posed.

But to acknoweldge them, as well as the hundreds of other "what ifs" you have not listed would be to become involved in a four hour program.

Our goal was to present a mere microscopic look at ways the "welfare system" is not working. We would hope that the program would help to inspire legislators and other officials to get crackin' on how to change it.

If you can find another way for us to say the word, "welfare" with<u>out</u> making you feel uncomfortable, I'd be happy to try it. It makes <u>me</u> feel uncomfortable saying it <u>any</u> way.

Dave Moore

6

Controversy

Minnesota Twins Baseball Club
Hubert H. Humphrey Metrodome
Minneapolis, Minnesota 55415
July 26th, 1983

Dear Dave:

I understand that you have not been to the Metrodome to see our Club play.

I would like to invite you and your wife to be my guests for dinner and a game before this Season is over.

Enclosed is a schedule. Please select the game you would like to see and give me a call.

Looking forward to hearing from you.

Sincerely,

Calvin

Calvin R. Griffith,
President

July 27, 1983

Mr. Calvin R. Griffith
President Minnesota Twins
Hubert H. Humphrey Metrodome
Minneapolis, Minnesota 55415

Dear Calvin,

As a baseball purist — perhaps even the most extreme of purists, considering your well documented history of battling some of the absurdities imposed on the game in recent years — I hope you'll forgive and understand my declining your kind invitation.

Calvin, I _have_ been in the Dome, and the experience left me so dispirited and sick-at-heart, that I simply cannot bear to watch a major league game in that place. My love for the game and its peculiarly romantic atmosphere and history, is so intense and dear to me, that I fear I would have to leave after the national anthem.

All of which, in no way, please understand, diminishes my affection for you or the team. I have personally cheered your defense of tradition, and your determination to fight the odds of today's self-serving ownerships.

And against my own personal predictions, the team is indicating its considerable talent; they've proven themselves a gallant bunch. In small strides they are gaining public respect, as they should.

I am sorry that financial considerations have taken you into the Dome. I'm sure you are no more fond of it than I.

Again, Calvin, thank you, but no thanks.

Gratefully,

Dave Moore

On February 8, 1982, an estimated three-to-four thousand people stood a dozen deep alongside the frontage road leading to the Carlton Celebrity Lounge in Bloomington, the very picture of the huddled masses, compressed as they were against one another to stave off a wind chill of minus forty-eight degrees. They had been gathering for hours awaiting the arrival of President Reagan and the opportunity to badger him with signs and banners about the oppressive interest rates that had kept so many of them in this land of plenty from buying homes and some of the luxury items to which Americans always feel entitled.

Inside the Carlton the industrial, political and social elite of the state Republican party also awaited the President. It was a high-test fund-raiser for Senator Dave Durenberger. Curt Beckmann of WCCO-Radio and I were selected to interview the President in a makeshift setting of an ante room adjacent to the ballroom.

Many viewers were put off, not by the substance of the interview as much as by its style.

February 10, 1982

Dear Dave:

For years, many years, you have been my favorite newscaster. Many times we have said, "They will never replace Dave Moore." Always interesting, always pertinent, and always worth hearing. Then came January 8, 1982.

On January 8th you had the privilege and honor of interviewing the President. You are the man I would have selected to do the interview, but Dave, I didn't like what you did. You seemed almost vindictive, as though you were out to get him. When you asked him questions it was as though you were badgering him. You kept dragging him back to the same question as though that were the only question that was important in this whole economic complex. Even your manner. You sat with your chin on your hand, your eyes squinted, as though you were watching for an openning to strike. It was not the Dave Moore that I know and like to see on the screen.

What happened? Were you overwhelmed by the fact that it was the President? Did you sink to the level of ordinary news people, thinking you might have a scoop and catch the President off guard by asking a question that he could not answer? I still think that Dave Moore is one of the best in the business, but this one really shook my faith and confidence. Perhaps I have been unfair in some of my accusations, and if that is true I am sorry. What is true is that this is the way it came across the screen to me, and that is the impression we live with.

Respectfully yours,

Mr. O. H.

115

February 12, 1982

Dear Mr. O. H.:

I am sorry my deportment during the interview with President Reagan has offended you.

In no way was my intention to disparage either the President or the office.

I asked him the question I perceived to be the question that the people would ask him: When might we expect some relief from high interest rates so that ordinary lending power might be made available to the people? When he failed to address the question, I tried to return him to it. Later he admitted there was no answer. I wasn't trying to trap him , nor was I at any time "vindictive."

We sometimes fail to realize that the President is our employee; we are his boss; we put him in the Presidency. He is responsible to us and when he wants to borrow ninety-one billion dollars I think he ought to have some answers for us.

My very physical position that seems to have annoyed you may be attributed to the fact that Mr. Reagan gives off a warm, comforting ambience, making one feel at home in his presence and not a need to sit at attention as though addressing a God.

The "squint" which also irritated you was not designed to "watch for an opening to strike," but rather a slight handicap over which I have no control.

Dave Moore

February 10, 1982

Mr. Moore:

I feel compelled to comment on your recent interview of President Ronald Reagan. Your treatment of President Reagan was unconscionable. Regardless of your political persuasion or philosophy, which I respect, he is our President, and was a guest in our State, and you had the honor of an exclusive interview — which by the way was the only reason I was tuned to WCCO in the first place.

President Reagan's expression was one of astonishment at your rudeness. Better manners are evidenced in the youth of today. It is too bad you didn't conduct yourself in as dignified a manner as your associate interviewer from WCCO Radio.

Since the President gave you the courtesy of an exclusive interview it seems that you could have extended the courtesy of a highly ethical journalistic interview in return.

I'm very grateful that by the flick of the dial I neither have to watch or listen to you present the news. I do not expect the courtesy of a reply.

Sincerely,

Helen Deardorff Robertson

February 12, 1983

Dear Ms. Robertson:

I am sorry you were offended by my deportment during the interview with President Reagan.

However, I am puzzled by your generalities:

I saw no evidence of the President's "astonishment at my rudeness." In what way was I not "highly ethical?"

Indeed, with the President, I was candid and specific. You have not shown that with me.

I simply asked the question which I thought the public might ask, for which I expected a specific answer. Later he admitted, honestly, there is no specific answer. Why could not that admission have come in response to my original question?

Four days after the fact I have received nineteen letters regarding the interview: fourteen have been positive. Yours is among the five complainants.

Sincerely,

Dave Moore

Dear Mr. Moore,

As a long time supporter and fan of WCCO News, I feel I must write this letter.

I was deeply disappointed in your interview with President Reagan this week. I felt you were repetitious and a "mite" hostile. I remember wondering why Curt Beckman was there, you did most of the talking. The real "corker" came after the telecast when you and Skip Loescher were discussing the program. Your first words were, "I really threw him a couple of zingers didn't I?" (Or words to that effect.) I had to rub my eyes and look again to see if that was really Dave Moore talking. What were you trying to do, make the President look stupid, or make yourself look clever? In my humble opinion your performance was "trite." I really enjoy and appreciate your sense of humor and the comradery with your news team. But I just had to tell you that this one time you really let me down.

Sincerely,

Mrs. Jerry Teig

Mrs. Jerry Teig

February 12, 1982

Dear Mrs. Teig,

I am incredulous! I cannot begin to believe — in fact in my wildest imagination it is absolutely incomprehensible to me that anyone, even the most humorless person in the entire world, could take my remark "I really threw him a couple of zingers..." as uttered in a serious vein!

It was a slight, off-hand, ad-libbed little throw-away remark. It wasn't meant to make myself "look clever" or to mock the Presidency...it wasn't even meant as humor. It was said in semi-satirical, self-ridiculing manner emphasizing the thoroughly unlikely position of a local yokel daring to question the President of the United States.

I was not "hostile" toward the President, I was not repitious; I merely wanted to get an answer, which, as an em-

ployee of the citizens of this country, I felt he was obligated to supply. You and I put him in that job, Mrs. Teig, and if he wants to borrow to pay off a ninety-two-billion-dollar debt, I think he better have some answers. That's our money — yours and mine.

Dave Moore

Feb 25, 1984

Dear Mr. Moore,

I have been a Minnesota resident for a little over four years, and in that time, I have come to look forward to the Channel 4 news. However, I do have a bone to pick with you, and I'll include the entire news staff of your station.

I like to watch professional wrestling. I don't pretend to believe that it isn't all faked. What I'd like to know is what gives you and Ralph Jon Fritz the authority to make fun of wrestlers and ridicule them and their way of earning a living? The way I see it, those people are entertainers, and what's wrong with giving us a laugh now and then?

I've never heard you say a derogatory word about Governor Perpich, Walter Mondale, or any other democrat. I've never heard a word from you about the fact that the Minnesota Democratic party lays false claims to being on the side of farmers and laborers, nor the myth that the Republican party in this state claims to be independent. Independent from what, does one dare ask?

Mr. Moore, you are entitled to your opinion, and I respect your rights. However, when you digress from your job of telling the news to run down an organized activity which draws more viewers than your newscasts, it tells me that you are not an unbiased reporter.

I don't suppose I'll ever know if you read this or not, as Cindy Bracatto won't be able to tell me, and you won't bother to answer. I've switched to Channel 5 in order to find a better alternative in the news and sports. I sincerely hope you either own most of WCCO or will make some changes, because I'd hate to see you get fired at your age.

A disgusted former viewer,

Bill Allen

Bill Allen

February 29, 1984

Dear Mr. Allen,

I am sorry that our wry observations on professional wrestling have offended you.

As a "straight man" for Ralph Jon or Mark Rosen, I have regarded my comments on the sport more as those of an observer rather than a reporter, and thus immune from the ethics of general reporting. I think we all accept the sport for the entertainment that it is and that any comments from me are not likely to either detract from the sport nor disturb its followers.

In your case I have erred and again, apologize for offending your sensibilities.

For the record, I niether own WCCO-TV nor regard my job as jeopardized.

All of us here have a profound respect for KSTP-TV News and I'm sure you, too, will find their work satisfactory.

Sincerely,

Dave Moore

Dave Moore

Dear Mr. Moore,

Your commentary on the individual arrested for violating the state statute against eating on an MTC bus was in very bad taste.

You implied that since the individual was only eating M&Ms that the arrest was an over-reaction to the situation, and that the individual should have been left alone to go his own way. For a person in your position to invite disrespect for the law is a disgrace.

Your sarcasm that what we may next have to fear is the eating of hamburgers and french fries on the buses only shows your ignorance of the situation.

Before this law was enacted people did eat and drink on the buses. And it was a mess. The floor of the buses were littered with the obvious; food containers and wrappers, pop cans and beverage containers.

It was the spilled food and drinks that was the real nightmare. On the seats as well as the floor. You could encounter catsup, mustard, onion, pickle, lettuce, tomato, beverages and ice cubes from discarded beverage containers. Ice cream! How would you like to slip on or sit on a dropped ice cream cone or spilled milk shake?

Before this law the buses were dirty, unsanitary and dangerous. And on a hot summer day they smelled.

As an MTC rider for fourteen years I can say that this law was the best improvement that has been made in that time. I think you owe the riders of MTC an apology for your comments.

Sincerely,

Wayne I. Bartell

Wayne I. Bartell

June 18, 1985

Dear Mr. Bartell,

Yes, I think you're probably correct.

I don't agree with you that my treatment of that news item was in bad taste. It wasn't that well done.

It was simply a dumb thing for me to do. It wasn't clever. The item itself was so lacking in substance that it failed to qualify for satire.

In twenty-eight years of reading the news on the air, I have committed many such indiscretions, and as a human I undoubtedly will commit others.

*I'm glad your perception caught me at it — it confirms
the bad taste I had in my mouth after reading the story.*

Dave Moore

As the give-away cheese program of a couple of years ran
down, Edina was included among those communities earmarked
for cheese handouts. Given that community's well known afflu-
ence, I referred to it as "designer" cheese.

Aug. 17, 1983

Dear Mr. Moore,

It seems no one is above taking their own cheap shots
at Edina generally, but your comment concerning "designer cheese" on the 10 pm news Tuesday, Aug. 16th was
a new low in contemporary poor taste. Your wit is increasingly sluggish and your tone condescending.

Surely it doesn't surprise you that your many neighbors in Edina are not all wealthy. Many work very hard to
remain in a suburb where their children can still receive a
superlative education. I know I've been doing it as a single
parent for eight years. And I now how weary Edina families are of the ancient chestnuts making Edina forever the
butt of so many ill-conceived Mpls. jokes. But to connect a
tasteless joke with any kind of food program today is
pompous, ridiculous and vulgar. Believe it or not, there are
hungry people in Edina, even some on AFDC. I've met some,
haven't you?

Perhaps people didn't line up in throngs to receive free
cheese in Edina. If we had, I can imagine what you would
have had to say about that.

Beware. Your audience is not as provincial as you think, Mr. Moore.

Good-bye Channel 4 News. Your last straw just broke this camel's back, and I will talk about you too.

Sincerely,

Joan Pudvan

Joan Pudvan

September 4, 1983

Dear Ms. Pudvan:

I am sorry the "designer cheese" reference offended you; sorry that your sensibilities preclude your acceptance of innocent social humor at the expense of your community.

Given their collective stature and sophistication, I don't believe residents of Edina, even the most witless among us, could possibly interpret the remark as a demeaning of welfare conditions or food programs.

You make the point yourself: our "audience is not provincial," otherwise I'm sure I'd have received more than your single protest.

I cannot finish this response. It was silly of me to have started it.

Suffice it to say that I accept your complaint, just as I hope you will accept my condolences,

Dave Moore

The following commentary was broadcast on our 5 PM Report, on the scene, at the opening of Canterbury Downs. The letter that follows (the writer's name is omitted at her request) was typical of several reacting to the reference to Lutherans. Considering the vast Lutheran populace of Minnesota, it was not a wise reference on my part. My response to this particular letter was made into a "form letter" to the others.

(PUSH TO ONE SHOT
OF DAVE)

I was 12 when my father returned
from his annual business trip to Chicago and reported that for the first
time he played the horses at Arlington
and won 10 bucks.

After a lengthy, colorful description of
his day at the track, my older brother
said, "I wish we had horse-racing
here!" "Never will," my father said.
"Why?" asked my brother. "Too
many Lutherans," said my father.

(ROLL VT NAT ALSO
MIX IN SHOT FROM
PADDOCK AND
SHELARD CHOPPER,
BUT KEEP
DAVE'S AUDIO)

So here we are, 45 years later —
horse racing in a state, where not only
(45 years ago) no stores were open on
Sundays, but George Nelson Dayton
covered the windows of his department store on Sundays. And as we
look out over the lush, pristine broad
expanse of these marvelous grounds,
we can't help but think of Jack Fena.
Jack Fena was a legislator from Hib-
bing whom God put on this earth to
get pari-mutuel betting into Minnesota. Time after time after time, Jack
brought the bill up in the legislature;
time after time it was laughed out of
committee ... stalled in the House ...
stalled in the Senate.

The big fear, of course, is that it would
bring the sleaze element to the track
... that low incomers would blow their
paychecks on lackadaisical nags with
such names as "Momma's Little Dar-
ling," "Heroic Prince" and "Bitty Bitty
Berta."

But if anyone *does* lose the home it
won't be entirely the fault of the Canterbury people. Never, in the history
of sport, have the promoters offered

the public such elaborate instruction on how NOT to lose ... not only on how not to lose, but how to dress, how to talk and where *not* to step.

I am ambivalent. I have no feelings about this adventure — one way or another — but I have to admit, it has two things going for it: the horses can eat the grass, and there's no roof over it.

And as far as the betting goes, let us all recall the last stanza of Damon Runyon's classic verse: I've seen 'em, these noble men ... up in the dough and out again. In fact, I've been there many-a-time myself ... And that's no joke. I've seen 'em in limousines ... With rocks on their dukes ... And dough in their jeans ... But they're all alike when they quite their scenes ... All horse-players die broke. Thank you.

June 29, 1985

Dear _____,

I was afraid I might, but I was hoping I wouldn't receive a single unhappy note about my reference to Lutherans.

I thought Lutheranism was so big that none of its practicioners could possibly be offended by a little jest.

It wasn't <u>meant</u> to be funny. It wasn't a joke. It was a remembrance of what my father actually said to me when I was twelve years old.

And he was right. The records will show that from the mid-twenties to the early fifties, Lutherans made up the largest single body politic in the state legislature.

I received one other letter in today's mail. It was from an associate pastor from the world's largest Lutheran con-

gregation in Minneapolis. It said, merely "Hooray for the Lutherans!"

Dave Moore

For the running of the first race at Canterbury, covered extensively by all four local channels, I announced that I had bet on a nag called, "Don's Wig." Almost as though the nag was playing into the joke, "Don's Wig," as I recall finished sixth out of a field of five! And of course thereafter, for the remainder of the broadcast, Ralph Jon Fritz and I made a big deal out of it.

7-8-85

Dear Mr. Moore,

It seems that I made you unhappy on the opening of "The Track."

You have made a number of remarks about me. You were unhappy that I didn't win, place or show. I don't even remember if I finished the race. It isn't easy to run and win a race without legs or feet. I just enter races and hope for a strong tail wind. Sorry I disappointed you.

DON'S WIG

Don's Wig

July 25, 1985

Dear Don's Wig,

Sorry I have been so late in responding to your kindness — but I have wanted to see how you did in later races.

The results of those races have indicated to me — in retrospect — that you did very well on that fateful opening day at Canterbury and I regret now that I so publically demeaned your alleged skills.

I thank you for your wig. It is in the capable hands of our Makeup department against the day when Bud Kraehling absolutely refuses to get off the air.

I am sure giving it up will prove an immense benefit to you: without all that hair flopping in your eyes you'll have an uncluttered view of all those horses-asses running in front of you.

Gratefully,

Dave Moore

June 9, 1983

Reid Johnson
News Director-WCCO
30 South 9th St.
Mpls, Mn. 55407

Dear Mr. Johnson:

This is a letter in regards to the comment that was made by WCCO's 10 O'Clock News anchorman, Dave Moore, on the night of Wed. June 8, 1983. The comment was made about and/or to newscaster Pat Miles.

The incident occured after Ms. Miles had interrupted Mr. Moore's final wrap-up, with a short acknowledgement of an event that gave recognition to the Women Leaders of the Twin City area. Mr. Moore was obviously perturbed by the interruption, as shown by his reaction. However, that situation, if needed, should have been handled behind the cameras, not in front. He followed with this *snide* and *sexist* comment:

"Give them an inch and they'll take the whole newscast."

As women and as watchers of WCCO's news, we felt outraged, appalled, and offended by this insulting, demeaning and very *patronizing* comment. Furthermore, it implied that he has the power and/or right to publicly undermine Ms. Miles' reporting.

It was a pleasure to see women get a truly-deserved recognition through the channels of commercial media, al-

127

beit, a tidbit amount. That Ms. Miles felt the need to interrupt the program to get the event covered, is indicative of the lack of equality in media coverage between women and men. We *applaud* Ms. Miles for having the courage to push forward with women's media coverage at the risk of "being a bad girl."

In summary, we hope that you, as News Director of WCCO, will take responsibility in exposing and confronting the discrimination that so blatantly was exposed by your anchorman, Dave Moore.

Sincerely,

M. C. S.

June 15, 1983

Dear Ms. S:

I can't believe it!

I simply can't <u>believe</u> it!

Please find attached a copy of the <u>scripted</u> (in other words, planned, contrived, premeditated) remarks which you found "patronizing" on June 8th.

Apparently my acting was too believable since you found me "obviously perturbed by the interruption, as shown by his reaction."

I cannot believe that the most insensitive, humorless, paranoid of righteous indignationists could not perceive that the entire sequence was a satire, or a play on chauvinism of the worst kind — particularly since it concerned a news item about women who have been recognized for their leadership in local business and civic affairs.

I have lost one dollar by your letter. One of our producers, having read the material, said, "Boy! Are you going to get complaints about this!"

To which <u>I</u> said: "I betcha' a buck I don't. The advancement of women is so established, it's so well recognized and understood and firmly implanted and acknowledged, that NO ONE would misunderstand the intent." (<u>un quote me</u>)

In a sense I was right. there was not one telephone call, not one card, not one letter from anyone who was "outraged" or "appalled."

In light of the very real and active progress that has been made in the past twenty-five years toward advancing the rights and equality of women, I suggest you re-evaluate your sensibilities in such a way that will help you understand that it's only those causes WITHOUT respect and support and credentials that CANNOT enjoy a jest at their own expense.

Sincerely,

Dave Moore

Bedtime Story

(PAT READS) (DAVE ON CAM) (DAVE & NEWSBOX — PAT LIVE)	Note: As Dave opens his mouth to speak, Pat interrupts ... Pat: Dave, if you don't mind ... I'll take the Bedtime Story tonight ... Dave: Well, that's fine ... but ...
(TAKE PAT FULL SCREEN NEWSROOM)	Pat: Because I was there at the Sheraton-Ritz tonight when
(TAKE NAT SOUND VTR REEL)	some 24 of the state's outstanding women, including Mercedes Bates,
(SUPER: SHERATON RITZ, MPLS)	the first woman elected vice president of General Mills, were honored for their achievements. Each of the 24 women, selected from all areas of Minnesota business and lifestyle, were featured in a series of full page ads created and produced by Powers. Tonight's program was sponsored by Working Opportunities for Women ... and Dave, I must tell you
(LIVE ON PAT)	it was quite an honor to M. C. an event

	with so many women leaders in this community ...
(PAT IN DAVE'S BOX)	Now Dave, you were saying?
(DAVE READS — TAKE WX ADDA FULL) Moore:	*(Grumbles ad-lib chauvinist remark)*

On December 31st, 1982 in the wake of a second deflation of the vaunted Humphrey Metrodome, and in a moment of misbegotten judgement, I chose to dramatize my displeasure with that facility by assuming the mantle of a cleric whom I named Brother Davidicus, from the Church of The Immaculate Deception. Early in the evening I was video-taped as the character outside the stadium, timing his remarks to coordinate with what would be my questioning of him, at ten o'clock, live, from my position at the anchor desk. Artistically it was artful. As a social commentary, it was a bomb. Here are two of the more literate of the fifty or so grievances received.

5 January 1983

Dear Mr Moore:

I've postponed writing you about the skit you did in a double role last week just so I could think a bit more moderately and perhaps more objectively. Whether it has helped is something maybe you will be the better judge about.

After the skit aired I called to speak with you about it, but you were taking no further calls I was told. Maybe I was not alone in objecting to the poor taste of the script. In short, I think I could illustrate my concern by a couple of parallel examples. I wonder if you would ever consider doing a "humorous" bit about the superintendent of the Minneapolis Public Schools and an alleged fondness for watermelon? Or perhaps describing a successful outing of the local B'Nai B'Rith as a "kike-hike?" Why not, it might get a few laughs? Well, if not then why not?

Your "take-off" on a most solemn Catholic doctrine, the Immaculate Conception, was really in extremely poor taste. I was offended by it, as were several others who watched your telecast. Perhaps Catholics do not enjoy the same fair shake at Channel 4 that Blacks and Jews do. I wonder why. I don't think it is anything malicious or even intentional. It is more likely just ignorance (from the Latin, don't know). The second part of P. T. Barnum's well known phrase is "..... and don't wisen-up a chump." Sir, I don't consider you a chump; I do hope some wisdom can be gained from this short piece of advice.

Sincerely,

R. L. Johnson

January 7, 1983

Dear Mr. Johnson:

If your displeasure by the "skit" of January 31st represents a consensus, then I probably have offended, equally, members of all religious persuasions.

But I think not. In addition to your letter, one other caller was similarly offended. There has been one letter of complaint, and another favorable. Four responses from an audience of more than one-hundred-thousand would seem to indicate a sense of public indifference to the matter. Apparently most people are assured that the Church is not likely to stand or fall by menial jibes put forth by me. After all, it survived more than a half century of George Bernard Shaw.

As I read along in your letter, I found myself sympathizing — not agreeing, but sympathizing — with certain of your points. Until your reference to the "kike-hike." At that point your credibility failed you.

To draw such an analogy is to be shallow and ludicrous. The "skit," in the final analysis, while its humor may be questioned, was niether mean nor name-calling in nature.

The word "kike" is a brutalizing and demeaning epithet, born of ignorance and cruelty.

But more disturbing to me than any of that — because who is to judge "taste?" — is that you were told that I was "not taking any phone calls." I take ALL phone calls at ALL times. Next time please insist on leaving your name and phone number, and you may use this letter as evidence of my sincerity.

Dave Moore

---

11 January 1983

Dear Mr Moore:

I appreciate your taking the time to reply to my letter regarding your "skit" of January 31st. It was good to learn that you do make yourself available to those who would try to reach you by phone.

Undoubtedly, you are a busy man and I don't propose a lengthy epistolary debate, but I do feel a few words of comment are in order on your letter. I was surprised primarily at its tone. You seem to have missed completely the point of my letter. In brief, I think it could be stated thus: you have indulged in a cheap ridicule of a Catholic doctrine for laughs. No one stated that your intention was to do this; I even suggested that it was all done out of ignorance. I asked rather rhetorically if you would consider a similar skit on a black theme and a Jewish theme. I suggested you would not. I asked why not. You venture no answer.

Mr Moore, I have black friends (one is also a Catholic). I have many Jewish friends (one is married to a Catholic). All tell me that they are getting used to material such as Archie Bunker uses (Coon, Wop, Polack,Heeb) , so your lecture came as something of a surprise ... I didn't suggest you use any of these epithets. My question was why don't you, since you apparently have an open season on Catholic themes.

This letter is already too long, but let me close with a comment on your apparent excuse for the whole incident.

You cite public indifference. You seem to feel that if four members of your audience out of one-hundred-thousand were offended that that hardly makes a case for bad taste. In your business, I suggest that four people who take the time to comment probably represent more like four-hundred viewers who were moved (pro or con) to register their views. I am really puzzled by your attitude, at least as I read it from your letter. Channel 4 is certainly not going to "do in" the Catholic church. That is not the point. Fairness and good taste are. Pontius Pilate could well ask "What is truth?," but I don't think Channel 4 can insouciantly ask as you do in your letter, "who is to judge taste?"

You goofed, Mr Moore.

Sincerely,

R. L. Johnson

---

11 January 1983

Dear Dave,

The other day, to my astonishment and complete disgust, I caught a brief reference in a program that you were doing to the "Church of the Immaculate *Deception*." I am sorry that I cannot anchor it more firmly in established fact regarding program, Bedtime Nooz, or what.

I am also very sorry that I heard you say it.

It is an obviously irreverent reference to one of our time-honored Catholic beliefs. I did a double-take when I heard it and could not let it pass unchallenged. I am not aware of an anti-Catholic bias on your part, but I think it may be beginning to show.

What did you mean by the reference? What was your intent? Why did you have to include such a blatant remark? I would appreciate a response from you.

You might give Garrison Keillor a call. He also made a reference of a similar nature, but his reference was much less derogatory.

Please, Dave, don't offend our beliefs and don't let your Catholic viewers harbor disdain for you.

Sincerely,

Fr. Ralph G. Zimmerman
Pastor
Immaculate Conception
Catholic Church

January 17, 1983

Dear Fr. Zimmerman,

I am sorry that my innocent effort to make a play-on-words has offended your sensibilities. Obviously it turned out to be a case of bad judgement on my part.

"Church of the Immaculate Deception" was an identification I gave to a church-like figure (played by myself) to carry out a good natured railing against the Metrodome; my feeling being that the Metrodome has turned out to be an immaculate deception, born not only from the fact that the public was given no say in its construction, but that it has not benfited either public or participants in the ways it was guaranteed to.

No malice toward the Catholic church or any church was intended. I have received just one other letter similar to yours. But, of course, since it offended any one person at all, I must regard the effort as a failure.

I am sorry for any embarrassment it may have caused you.

Sincerely,

Dave Moore

July 18, 1984

Dear Dave:

During your broadcast of Friday's, July 13th, "10:30 p.m. Report," you commented to the effect that rodeos are a good form of entertainment. I would like to dispute this by filling you in on a few facts.

The animals used for rodeos are very docile creatures. These are not the days of the "Old West" where animals were tamed in the wild. In order to provoke these animals into a frenzied state, they are struck with electric prods, their tails are docked, and a strap is harnessed tightly across their genitals; the latter causing permanent damage. As for the calves that are roped, they are thrown into the side walls so hard that their shoulders and ribs are broken, and these injuries go untreated.

Rodeos, circuses, zoos and horseracing, to mention a few, are all forms of exploiting animals for entertainment. This would be an excellent topic for WCCO to cover, one that would greatly inform the public, and one that would hold their interest. If you have any questions or would like more information, please contact me or the Animal Rights Coalition.

Sincerely yours,

Paula Weiner

July 20, 1984

Dear Ms. Weiner,

I didn't think I could be guilty of such an insensitive remark — even in an ad-lib situation — about rodeos.

I think they're barbaric and I didn't think I could suddenly become so unacquainted with that feeling.

I have just viewed the tape of last Friday's 10PM newscast: you are guilty of mis-listening.

This is what happened: immediately following the footage on the rodeo (with Ralph's narration) Ralph appeared on the screen to re-cap the Twins game at the Metrodome,

*to which I said, (Quote) "What a rewarding performance
for thirty thousand spectators!"*

*There was nothing said whatsoever in reference to the
rodeo. You are not altogether at fault: it is the nature of
the beast of television news programs, the various items of
which are connected by improptu, thoughtless, idle banter
between the participants that requires the viewer — in a
relaxed, tranquil, casual environment — to exercise rapt
attention. It is a situation that, more often that not, pro-
duces mis-interpretation.*

Sincerely,

Dave Moore

*PS: Please understand that your admirable effort to illu-
minate me on the sins of the Rodeo, has not been lost on
me. I have shared your letter with others here.*

1/10/84

Dear Dave:

Your closing news item concerning Edmund D. Looney,
who changed his name because he planned to go into psychiatry, is about twenty-five or twenty-seven years too
late.

Ed Looney was a graduate student several years behind
me in the Psychology Department at Yale. After complet-
ing his Ph.D. in about 1957 or 1958 (possibly 1959), he decided to go to medical school, and changed his name for the
reason you cited to Lowney. The last I heard, he was a professor, not of Psychiatry, but dermatology at the University of Michigan. I can't imagine where you obtained this
"news" item. It was reported at the time in a *Time Magazine* column entitled "People and Places", or something
like that, but I don't suppose you or your writers cull old
Time isues for current news, even of the humorous
variety.

Best regards,

Warren W. Roberts

January 13, 1984

Dear Mr. Roberts,

I know the world is getting smaller, but this is ridiculous!

You are absolutely correct: the item about Edmund Looney, did, indeed, come from a Miscellany column of an old Time Magazine — 1956, as I recall.

On that particular night I had prepared a final item for the newscast which I had to discard at the last second because the video tape, which was necessary to tell the story, turned out to be faulty.

I was told of this during a commercial break in the news, and hastily grabbed the Looney item from a reserve file I keep in a desk drawer.

But I certainly should have labeled it for the vintage item it was.

But let me confirm your correct presumption: we do not cull old issues of magazines to get our news.

I am delighted to have your letter, thank you.

Dave Moore

Dear Sir

I See You Ever Night at 5 You Tell Us To Buckle Up

I am 81 Year Old I Have Never Buckle Up I Drive So That I Dont Need A Belt I Wish That You Would Tell All The People To Drive So That They Dont Need A Belt If You Road Witch Me You Would Not Need A Belt

Frank Jones

May 28, 1986

Dear Mr. Jones:

Your note has touched the curiosity of all of us.

We are having some difficulty envisioning how you

137

might drive so that you "don't need a belt."
    Do you drive on roads untraveled by other vehicles?
    Is it that you travel at such a slow rate of speed that when you spot a potential collision you can jump out?
    I should be happy to have you enlighten me further, Mr. Jones. Meantime, I think it best that you drive alone.

Dave Moore

Dear Dave,
    I am directing this note to you as the senior news broadcaster in the twin cities and as such hope you can influence the others by example.
    I am concerned with the phrase "claimed responsibility" used in reporting various terrorist activities. I feel the phrase grants too much credence to the terroists methods and also is a trite, unthinking expression. Further, the word "responsible" loses the dignity normally associated with it.
    As an alternate I should like to suggest "admitted complicity" as an more appropriate phrase. Better yet, perhaps you and your associates could make improvements which would convey a sense of outrage to your listeners and still not be accused of editorializing.
    Sincerely,

R.C. Kelly

✉

January 11, 1985

Dear Mr. Kelly,
    I have been sitting here with your letter before me all these weeks waiting for divine or professional inspiration to guide me to something more appropriate than either "claimed responsibility" or "admitted complicity."

138

The latter is a nice phrase but I think it a bit fanciful. And while it may be "trite" (as you say) I don't feel the former is an "unthinking expression." There can be no doubt as to its meaning.

I feel the word, "admitted" connotes contrition, even shame, almost synonymous with "confess," when it should convey a feeling of boastfulness. These terrorists are just as proud of their actions as you are incensed by them. Nor do I detect a sense of the editorial (as you have implied) in "claimed responsibility."

However, since it is so pleasing to hear from one who is particular about the care and maintenance of language, I defer to you: the next time the choice is presented, I'll select "admitted complicity."

I hope to hear other suggestions from you; God knows I try, but we do get awfully slothful here at times.

Sincerely,

Dave Moore

7

Kudos

I approach this segment with some degree of frustration because I have misplaced my replies to three of the most flattering letters. There is some comfort in knowing that Ms. Wilson, Mr. Farley and Mrs. Auger, at least, have the replies, or, I'm sure, have read them.

Memory does not serve me back to the 1967 date of Mr. Farley's letter. I assume that the "apparently extemporaneous remarks on bigotry" to which he refers were made during the course of one of the Saturday Night Bedtime programs, since it was the only forum available to me for making such comment. My head would have rolled, justifiably, had they been made in a formally scripted Six or Ten O'Clock newscast.

July 30, 1967

Dear Dave:

I have been sitting in front of the typewriter for five minutes trying to compose succinct, punchy phrases of commendation for your apparently extemporaneous remarks on bigotry at 1:10 A.M. today. I have had little success with the phrases and will have to resort to something more prosaic.

Dave, I have never heard a more forthright unequivocal denunciation of bigotry on TV. The thing I am having difficulty with is trying to say that you didn't have to say it. It was, apparently, from the heart. Without meaning to be sloppy about it, one would expect to hear such phrases from some members of the cloth or true leaders in the area of propagating human dignity. Dave, it was, simply, great. I literally cheered. Hopefully, within our lifespan such views will be dominant and popular. Then those of us who lucked out with white skins in a white society will have one real area of which to be proud. Thank you!

Eugene W. Farley

In 1977 Anita Bryant had cause a stir with her nation-wide campaign against homosexuality. One particular "Moore on Sunday" public affairs program had to do with the prospect of St. Paul voters invoking a so-called Gay Rights Ordinance whereby St. Paul homosexuals would be deprived of their basic civil rights as applied to housing, education and employment. We closed the program with the comment: "To Anita Bryant and to whomever else has worked to reverse the civil rights of another citizen, we say, 'You ought to be ashamed; you simply ought to be ashamed.'"

The program, entitled "Fair Game Faggot," inspired a torrent of lively outrage and abuse unparalleled in its creativity. The following two letters are exemplary.

Nov 2, 1977

Dear Dave,
I don't know how tenuous your position at WCCO is because of the stand you have taken against bigotry and intolerance.

I do want you to know that I have seen both of the last two 'Moore of Sunday' programs, and I think you are a very courageous man. I agree completely with everything you said, but it's one thing for me to tell you I believe as you do, and it's another thing for you to put yourself out there on the line. I can imagine all the crazy, narrow-minded people who must have written you hate mail, and who must have demanded that you be fired.

I know the response has been running against you. I suppose it is some consolation for you to know that you *are* right in your analysis of the present movement to deny civil rights to lesbians and gay men.

I feel frightened, because I think we are outnumbered. I don't understand all the crazy fear on the other side, which borders on fanaticism. I am now reading John Toland's biography of Hitler, and I feel disquieted by the similarity between the rise of Naziism and the rise of Anita. Both movements seem based on negatives: both are rooted in hatred and illogic. Both movements are emotionally based on incorrect assumptions about the nature of Jews and homosexuals. Both seem to involve some kind of mass scapegoating.

So, you have put yourself in a very vulnerable position by taking on this movement. All I can say is that I am very moved by your courage. You risked a lot. It's so rare that I feel this kind of admiration for someone.

Good luck to you. If they try to get rid of you on WCCO, I'll be the first contributor to the Dave Moore Defense Fund.

Sincerely,

M. Sue Wilson

Dear Mr. Moore,

This letter to you is perhaps a delayed reaction to your show that interviewed some homosexual individuals in our area. When I saw a few days later some of the hysterical reactions to that show I knew I must add my opinion.

Perhaps the disheartening political events of this past week helped me crystallize my feelings. How can a television show about love, in whatever form it takes, get such a gut reaction when all around us is dishonesty, greed, warfare and human misery? No one seems to stand up and say "Hey, whats wrong with all of us?"

I suppose I really want to express my feelings to those that decide your program policies. I sincerely hope that they allow such controversial subjects to be dicussed.

It might be of interest to you to know that my five grade-school age children watched that show with me. They were allowed to stay up late that night because some of them had been filmed at the smoking clinic that was to be shown on the consumer reports section that night. Two of them continued playing chess throughout the show glancing only occasionally, the other three seemed a little surprised at some scenes but certainly not shocked or revolted. It seems to me that opening such a topic for discussion gave me the opportunity to help my children to view this way of life with compassion and understanding not revulsion and fear. I guess that I viewed that feature as being about love and since when is love a dirty word.

Sincerely,

Mrs. Mary Dee Auger

When one has been on the air as long as I have been, sometimes letters re-surface. In the case of the following two gentlemen, I was glad to be re-united through our correspondence.

January 21, 1986

Dear Dave:

Please accept my sincere thanks for having been a guest on *Campus Closeup*. It was the quickest thirty minutes I've spent on or off camera. You are a fascinating human being. I hope you decide to go ahead with your plan to write that book of letters. I believe people really will be interested in your interactions with others.

I looked through my files and found the letters we exchanged some seven and a half years ago... nice to know that I was right then and right now. Thanks again for your kindness for being on *Campus Closeup*. I hope we can meet again.

Best Regards,

Richard L. Holloway, Ph.D.

January 24, 1986

Dear Dick,

I think probably you have just secured your position in the book, should it ever come about.

Modesty may preclude my doing so; on the other hand, a resumption of correspondence that began nine years before the fact might tie-in appropriately with the very reason for the book: the kinds of relationships that a newscaster establishes with his viewers.

I am quite touched by the very fact that you have saved the 1977 letter.

Later I told Janis Pettit (ed. note: program producer) of the great opportunity I missed with you: I don't know why it failed to occur to me that the very problem I discribed on the air — establishing curricula, shaping it and adhering to it (grading?) is precisely the kind of work you do!!

I can't imagine your doing it any better than you interview. I've never spent such a speedy thirty minutes in my life!

Dave Moore

November 18, 1977

Dear Mr. Moore

I was present at your breakfast for the Edina Colonial Church this morning, and I would like to share with you my feelings as I left that gathering.

My wife and I moved to Minnesota last year from New York, and needless to say, a major move like that caused me some apprehension. Our final stop before arriving in the Twin Cities was the Eau Claire, Wisconsin Holiday Inn. You, Bud Kraehling, and Susan Spencer provided me with my first glimpse of life in Minnesota. So, I feel a special warmth for you and the job you do. Before I met many people in this new setting, yours was a "friendship" on which I relied.

Although I feel good about telling you this, I can appreciate the kind of burden a person in your position must bear. Not only are you expected to be knowledgeable and credible, but you are expected to be a friend to your viewing audience as well. As you spoke on Friday morning , I sensed that the human burden was one with which you feel more comfortable.

So, not as a comment on your credibility (which is high) but as a human being, your impact was strong. Rather than teaching me more about the news I learned more about ourselves as humans with hearts.

Thank you, Dave Moore, for being a warm, kind, and most of all, a sharing individual.

Sincerely,

Richard L. Holloway, Ph.D.

November 23, 1977

Dear Dr. Holloway,

I cannot begin to tell you how touched I am by your thoughtful note.

In recent years I have been loathe to make the kinds of appearances I did last Friday since it has always been dif-

146

ficult for me to gauge the collective temperament of an audience, and of course out of fear that I shall either be (1) too expansive, (2) not expansive enough, (3) incapable of supplying the proper information (4) likely to respond trivialy to a seriously intended question, or (5) all of the above.

Within thirty seconds of the time I launched my rambling, I felt altogether at ease — because I sensed the warmth and genuinely supportive nature of the group. Your kindly letter reflects that warmth.

Your letter has reminded me that I must write a nice letter to someone today.

Gratefully,

Dave Moore

2/14/85

Dear Dave Mr. Moore

So, you are retiring from the 10 o'clock news! I have been reading the paper and thinking about all the nice things they are saying about you. Do you know what? I think its the truth! I started to dig through some of my old college "stuff" and I found one of my most treasured possessions — "A letter From Dave Moore." I wrote it when I was a Freshman and have kept it all these years (copies attached). As you can see my handwriting has not improved dramatically. Anyway, I was and still am impressed with the Fact that you took the time to answer the letter of an eighteen-year-old student. It was a thrill then and it was tonite when I showed it to my eleven year old daughter. Even she was impressed. As the paper said you are like Family. Thats how I feel and I just wanted to say thanks for taking the time to write a letter, being Funny on the Bed Time Newz, and being a part of the Minn-er-so-ta traditions.

Pat Spellacy

Pat Spellacy

11/17/66

Dear Mr. Moore,

I just had to write. I just have to tell someone about our mattresses. I am going to school at St. John's University in Collegeville & we had some old beds with poor mattresses. So they said, they would get us some new ones. We were hoping they would be Sealy Posture Pedic & sure enough our wish came true. Boy, is it heavenly! Just like sleeping on a Cloud. I have to get three guys to drag me out of bed in the morning because I am sleeping so soundly. Well, I have to go now, because its getting late (already 7 o'clock) & I want to enjoy my new mattress as much as possible.

Your well rested friend.

Pat Spellacy

Pat Spellacy

P.S. The Shirts beat the Skins up here again (406-71) but that's because the skins star center Clyde Clomfoot had a sore back. (He didn't get a Sealy Posture Pedic)

November 19, 1966

Dear Pat:

Wonderful!

Thank you so much. So proud and delighted was I with your note, I handed it over Mr. Ted Deutsch, the sales manager of the Sealy Company. I happened to have been with him at the time your letter reached me.

He xeroxed it three times to show HIS employers. I hope you are not offended by this show of presumptuousness.

Were the truth known, we do not intend, on the Bedtime News, to SELL Sealy Posturepedic mattresses. Our job is to call the public's attention to Sealy...of course, when the public buys BECAUSE of what they have heard on the Bedtime News, that's nice, too.

Thank you again, Pat, for taking the time to write. Letters such as yours certainly help to ease jobs such as mine.
Gratefully,

Dave Moore

And, then, the following letter which defies classification but gave me personal satisfaction.

3/18/86

Dear Mr. Dave Moore:

My wife & I used to like very much when you and Bud, were together on the six oclock news, Wish it were that way again.

Dave I have seen you many times for years.

I know how you love baseball, and you know the game well. I played semi-Pro ball years ago.

Going to Nicollet ball park, or Lexington ball park, sometimes in morning and afternoon. It's a damn shame to sit in the Dome, for baseball; Twins' aren't going any place, I know.

My friend Eugene (Gene) Trow died from cancer. I don't feel sorry for my self, I am damn mad I lost my Voice box, due to cancer. How I love people and baseball.

Sincerely!

Leonard (Link) Peterson

March 20, 1986

149

Dear "Link,"

Thanks for the nice letter.

One of the joys of working as a native son in this business is the mail that brings remembrances of another day in the Twin Cities.

Your very mention of Lexington and Nicollet ball parks restores for me many pleasant moments of my boyhood.

I remeber Gene Trow well: over the past years, before his illness, I'd stop in at Farmers/Mechanics bank to visit with him.

Recently I had the pleasure of meeting Larry Rosenthal and Leo Wells — Leo's well-recovered from some very complicated heart surgery of last year.

So, with a voice-box you can't cheer? Anyone can cheer. You do it with your mind.

Dave Moore

8

Reflections

Writing has never come easy for me. It has always been a long, tedious, painstaking process. In our newsroom our editors and reporters turn out five pieces of copy, each, in the time it takes me to complete one. Of all the professionals in the world, those I admire most are writers. How, in Heaven's name do Klobuchar and Soucheray and Grow turn out a column a day? How does Nick Coleman turn out the volumes he does? How did George Rice and Al Austin grind out editorial thought each day? Not just grind it out, one word after another, but develop it so that the humor and philosophy and sensitivity stream into a literary flow and become a very nice thing indeed.

For me this volume has been a labor of love without time or editorial constraints. But still, it has not come easy.

With that as a background you can appreciate how panic seizes me when, on those rare occasions, my superiors ask me to provide a commentary on one of the newscasts.

Two of them, and a "Letter To The Editor" of the *Minneapolis Star and Tribune* follow.

Briefly

TO THE EDITOR: Some time ago the *Star's* editor asked its readers, "Well, how do you like Briefly, the new feature on page one of the *Star*?"

Well, I don't like it. It disappoints me. My objection has nothing to do with *The Star's* stealing television's thunder — although I suspect deep in my subconscious there are some sour grapes.

On those rare occasions when I am invited to address an organization the question arises concerning the "competition" between the press and television news. I do my best to explain that save for the battle to get the advertising dollar, in no other way can the two media be competitive. We feel our prime duty, in our limited time on the air, is to report the essential — and frequently just the bare facts — of a story, trusting the viewer to go to the newspaper for background and the underlying significance.

But now the newspaper comes along and says: "We know you are busy, busy people who do not have the time (or can't be bothered) with background and significance, so we're just going to skim off the top for you."

I fear and deplore those statistics that tell us more people get their news from television than from any other source. I think this reflects a lazy, slothful, uninterested, and, given time, an ignorant and uncomprehending public.

The reasoning advanced on behalf of Briefly embraces many sound and well-taken points, but fails to convince me that the very concept is not symptomatic of a creeping, mass inertia.

Briefly's very excellence compounds the threat. It is very well done. It is inviting. It is precise and thoughtful. But by no means can it be comprehensive, just as television news, through lack of manpower and time, cannot be comprehensive.

I guess what I'm trying to say is the television news *must* be Briefly. The press is not so obligated and by imposing this concept on itself, not only is it encouraging the public to read briefly, but to think briefly.

Goodbye to the Met

This used to be our favorite time of the year for watching the Twins: generally they were out of the race by now, the pressure off and they were playing reasonably well. But today the notes and tones of this September song are dissonant and off-key.

The sorrow that is visiting so many of us rigid, inflexible purists on this day comes not just from the thought of the Twins playing baseball in a building — but they're going to tear this place down! This stadium, one of the three best in the world, this last bastion of baseball stability, is only twenty-five years old!

Tearing it down and replacing it with an antiseptic, plastic, marketing and housing complex is another loss for the preservation of history — another victory for industrial greed. And next year this beloved baseball team will be playing out its comic opera in a convention hall that stands as a monument to man's fascination for the vulgar and tacky.

But they can't tear down the memories. I was here the day Earl Battey was thrown out on a single to right; the day Richie Allen legged out two inside-the-park homeruns.

You know, it was Richie Allen who said of artificial turf, "If a horse can't eat it, I ain't playin' on it." There was the day, just last year, when Mike Cubbage hit for the cycle. I was here.

And all of those sun-splashed days, with Killebrew at bat, when the pitchers couldn't keep the ball out of Harm's way.

And poor Willie Norwood out there in center field: one of his replacements, after stumbling around out there, said, "Norwood's got that field so screwed up, no one can play out there!"

Game's over now. I'm just going to sit here for a few minutes — and weep.

January 28, 1986

On this date, before the eyes of the world, the space ship, Challenger, blew up over the Atlantic Ocean. Our News Director, Reid Johnson, asked me to provide a commentary that would describe the sudden change in ambience in our newsroom, remindful of the pall that took over twenty-three years earlier when President Kennedy was assasinated.

So many of us in this business, which, more often than not, is the business of Dread and Disaster, like to think that our long-standing professionalism renders us impervious to catastrophe.

How short our memories. How painfully short was defined for us today when we walked into our work atmosphere, our *professional* work atmosphere, to one sadly reminiscent twenty-three years ago to learn that our President had been shot to death in Texas and television allowed the entire country to be numbed together.

Then, as now, the immediate ambience was not one of grief — the shock was still too fresh for that — but one of contained activity: people going about their work, distractedly. No little pockets of people joking, laughing. No hollering across the room. No *dashing* across the room, video tape in hand, to make a deadline. Each of us working at imperviousness, containment.

You may not recognize it, but just as you do, when we read you the news each night, we empathize with the meatpackers and their employers in Austin ... we agonize with the farmer in fear of losing his land. The appalling events of Madison, Wisconsin (Ed Note: U of M athletes in rape case) have cut deep into our pride and shattered our spirit for sport — and perhaps, most painful of all, raised the level of bigotry that's inherent in all of us.

Why, has what happened today, dropped *those* events — far closer to our hearts than Cape Canaveral and the space program — into a diminished perspective?

Because as a nation we saw this happen — together. Right there. On the spot. A wonderfully spirited, loving, almost saint-like New Hampshire school teacher, before the very eyes of her entire country, blown away from us forever. All in the name of progress.

Why that monster exploded, what went wrong, means nothing to us now. Each of us, including the professional couriers of Disaster and Doom, is thinking: Why? Why, in God's name, are we doing this? Is this Progress?

That's what we're thinking now.

In time, as time has a way of doing, we'll recover our sensibilities and recognize that yes, yes that's progress — and there are some, as many, many others have — who die for it.

And once again, as the years intervene, we'll find ourselves impervious to catastrophe. Until the next time.

Goodbye at Ten

In a sense, has this not turned out to be a two-pronged biography? Of a profession and a career?

If so I must include two moments — on September 17th and December 14th, 1985 — which I dearly wish to retrieve — and bury. Together they would seem to represent a lesson in human frailty from which all of us can learn: our personal vulnerability can be most telling in those areas where we feel the strongest.

My departure from the 10 PM Report in September, after twenty eight years, had been announced loudly and proudly and well in advance. On February 14th Nick Coleman and the *Minneapolis Star/Tribune*, in what I deem one of the most personally gratifying cases of editorial misjudgement in the history of local journalism, laid out my entire career on two full pages of the front section of the newspaper, and continued the glorification in the Variety section. Rick Shefchik did the same in the *St. Paul Pioneer Press and Dispatch*. Sleep-crusted eyes must have told the collected citizenry, taking the paper from its doorstep, that I had died. Indeed, Mrs. Moore sent her daughter into our bedroom to check. In the days soon thereafter two of my personal idols, Jim Klobuchar and Joe Soucheray added laudatory columns.

Our General Manager, Ron Handberg had not relished the anticipation of suggesting my time had come at ten o'clock. The twenty years Ron and I had worked together in our cluttered newsroom transcended the bonds of casual friendship which may have grown even stronger as he advanced from reporter to Associate News Director to News Director to WCCO-TV's General Manager. The exquisite nature of the friendship was such that he took no punitive action in the case of my loathsome DWI charge. It was a well publicized charge that might have brought suspension, if not total dismissal by most employers. Ron recognized, apparently, that personal remorse and anguish was penalty enough.

Weeks before our meeting on the matter of relinquishing the 10 PM Report, I had all but convinced myself that the nights, at long last, were beginning to take their toll, that the time had come for a change. Our thinking was blessedly meshed.

Ron had decided on a gala celebration of the event for September 17th at the Carlton Celebrity Lounge. Hundreds of invitations were accepted including those by long-time co-workers who had advanced to CBS News.

I put this down on paper with Roget's Thesaurus at hand. It is useless to me. I find no words in that thumb-worn book to describe my feelings on that proud and humbling, rapturous and embarrassing, wonderful and awful evening. Suffice it to say that when it came time for me to offer my acknowledgement and thanks — Zilch. Nothing.

I was as bereft of word then as I am now in recalling it all. Six months of preparation — nothing on paper, only in the mind — for that glorious moment had left me. How many times in those six months, driving northbound and southbound on 35W, had I delivered that speech? But on the scene, that night, after recalling wonderful moments of newsroom life, anecdotage and joke, I numbed. Hardly a smidgin of acknowledgement of the good fortune and good people who had made my longevity possible. Only numbness.

It happened again on December 14th: thirty-five years of addressing audiences; a practiced ad-libber, glib of tongue, quick
with the repartee, the bon mot ever at hand. Zilch. Nothing.

The occasion was the company Christmas party, which I had
been asked to emcee. But for this moment, unlike the September
evening, I was totally unprepared. Following a magnanimous introduction of me by Ron Handberg, my fellow workers arose and
applauded, deafeningly. To this courtesy my response was to assume a comatose state of such proportion as to send the most
learned doctors scrambling for back issues of the American Medical Journal. If there is a God why couldn't She have supplied me
with something! anything! to thank all those wonderful people for
helping to make one person's work so fulfilling and enduring?
Zilch. Nothing.

Since there is no retrieving either of those regretful moments,
I beg your patience here to offer a transcript of a last goodbye on
the 10 PM Report on September 20th.

Each time I try to make this point I am charged with false modesty. It is a point I should have made last Tuesday night at the Carlton Lounge, but I was in such a state of emotional upheaval I had
not the wherewithal to put it altogether.

The point is this: one does not survive twenty eight years at
this news desk on one's talents alone. You have to have help from
two sources: you have to have a supportive employer, and you
have to have a loyal audience. My longevity, I am happy to tell
you, is a result of having been blessed with both. I have survived
all these years in this high transiency business because my employers have refused to measure my worth by the fallacious standards of the so-called audience rating system, in my view one of
social history's classic shams — a hoax of such insidious dimen-
sion as to produce this circumstance in our community:

A newscaster who has proved her skills and credibility beyond all doubt is suddenly instructed to alter her personality to ac-

comodate the style of her co-worker and the whims of her audience with which her employer pretends familiarity. We must not disparage this very qualified newscaster's compliance with the order, but rather that her employer had the temerity and gracelessness to even suggest such a change. It is a loathesome work condition that underscores my own good fortune.

Under two managements over these twenty-eight to thirty-five years, at no time has any executive here so much as hinted that my job might be at stake because of failing ratings. Employers such as mine are what keep audiences such as you, and I thank God for the both of you.

Also do not worry about the future state of this news program. Columbia University, Dupont, and Peabody people have already recognized Don Shelby as an exceptionally gifted journalist. And this one (Ed. note: referring to Pat Miles) has had your solid approval now for three years. For the last three months she has been carrying more than her share of the load, literally speaking, and as soon as she drops that bomb (Ed. note: gives birth) she'll be in good shape for the rest of us. I leave you in excellent hands.

Afterword

I have reserved this final page to recall a moment of last year which I hope will serve as an ever-lasting reminder to both the neophyte and experienced professional that in this business, where praise and adulation and high pay abound, the individual is never nearly as important, or as critical to the cause as he would like to think.

When I called the University of Minnesota athletic ticket office to inquire of my chances of buying tickets to a Wisconsin-Illinois football game to be played at Champaign, Illinois, I asked to speak to Ken Buell, the ticket manager.

"May I tell Mr. Buell who is calling?" said the young lady on the other end of the line.

"This is Dave Moore."

Ken Buell came to the phone and said, "I must tell you of an amusing thing that just happened." He explained that his office does business with Dave Moore, who is the operations manager of the Minnesota Twins. He had asked the young lady, "Which Dave Moore? Is it THE Dave Moore?"

"No," she said, "It's the one on television."